Soviet Union in World War 2

A Captivating Guide to Life in the Soviet Union and Some of the Main Events on the Eastern Front Such as the Battle of Stalingrad, Battle of Kursk, and Siege of Leningrad

© Copyright 2020

All Rights Reserved. No part of this book may be reproduced in any form without permission in writing from the author. Reviewers may quote brief passages in reviews.

Disclaimer: No part of this publication may be reproduced or transmitted in any form or by any means, mechanical or electronic, including photocopying or recording, or by any information storage and retrieval system, or transmitted by email without permission in writing from the publisher.

While all attempts have been made to verify the information provided in this publication, neither the author nor the publisher assumes any responsibility for errors, omissions or contrary interpretations of the subject matter herein.

This book is for entertainment purposes only. The views expressed are those of the author alone, and should not be taken as expert instruction or commands. The reader is responsible for his or her own actions.

Adherence to all applicable laws and regulations, including international, federal, state and local laws governing professional licensing, business practices, advertising and all other aspects of doing business in the US, Canada, UK or any other jurisdiction is the sole responsibility of the purchaser or reader.

Neither the author nor the publisher assumes any responsibility or liability whatsoever on the behalf of the purchaser or reader of these materials. Any perceived slight of any individual or organization is purely unintentional.

Free Bonus from Captivating History (Available for a Limited time)

Hi History Lovers!

Now you have a chance to join our exclusive history list so you can get your first history ebook for free as well as discounts and a potential to get more history books for free! Simply visit the link below to join.

Captivatinghistory.com/ebook

Also, make sure to follow us on Facebook, Twitter and Youtube by searching for Captivating History.

Contents

- FREE BONUS FROM CAPTIVATING HISTORY (AVAILABLE FOR A LIMITED TIME) 1
- INTRODUCTION 1
- CHAPTER 1 – BEFORE THE WAR 3
- CHAPTER 2 – STALINISM 8
- CHAPTER 3 – 1938 AND 1939 15
- CHAPTER 4 – INTERLUDE 24
- CHAPTER 5 – BARBAROSSA 27
- CHAPTER 6 – WAR OF EXTERMINATION 33
- CHAPTER 7 – THE MAJOR BATTLES 45
- CONCLUSION 75
- BIBLIOGRAPHY .... ERROR! BOOKMARK NOT DEFINED.

Introduction

One can bear anything, the plague, hunger and death, but one cannot bear the Germans. One cannot bear these fish-eyed oafs contemptuously snorting at everything Russian. We cannot live as long as these grey-green slugs are alive. Today there are no books, today there are no stars in the sky, today there is only one thought: Kill the Germans. Kill them all, and dig them into the earth. Then we can go to sleep. Then we can think again of life, and books, and girls, and happiness. We shall kill them all. But we must do it quickly or they will desecrate the whole of Russia and torture to death millions more people.

   –Excerpt from an article in the Soviet paper Red Star *(Krasnaya Zvezda) by writer Ilya Ehrenburg*

No nation suffered more losses during the Second World War than the Soviet Union. The figure most historians recognize as roughly accurate is twenty million. The exact figure is impossible to tally for a number of reasons: destroyed records, inexact pre-war records, Soviet politicization of the population figures before and after the war, and much more. No matter what the exact total was, what is known is that the Soviet population only recovered its losses from the war in the late 1950s.

For those of you unfamiliar with WWII, the combined losses sustained by the United States and Great Britain were just over 800,000 dead. The Soviets lost that many people during the Siege of Leningrad alone.

This is an introduction to life in the Soviet Union right before and during the war. This e-book is meant as a brief overview and introduction to World War II on the Eastern Front. At the end of the book, you will find a short list of some of the thousands of books and articles available on the subject, which will help give you a much deeper understanding of this tragic but fascinating subject.

Chapter 1 – Before the War

In 1917, the Bolshevik ("majority") wing of the Russian Social Democratic Labor Party staged a revolution that established communism as the system of government in the capital city of Petrograd (it was later known as Leningrad from 1924 to 1991 and is known as St. Petersburg today). The revolution quickly spread to Moscow, and in a short period of time, the Bolsheviks (known as the "Reds" for their banners, which were red for the color of the workers' blood) and the Whites (for the color of royalty, as they supported the old aristocratic regime led by the tsar and his family, the Romanovs) were at each other's throats.

Between 1918 and 1922, the Red and White Armies fought a bloody civil war, which cost millions of lives. During the conflict, the Bolsheviks executed the tsar and his family and eventually emerged victorious. The world had its first communist government.

Leading this new government was Vladimir Lenin, the organizer of the revolution and the political theorist behind the Communist Party of the Soviet Union (CPSU), which was what the Bolsheviks had evolved into. Lenin's ideas were based on the readings and beliefs of the German political philosopher Karl Marx (1818-1883) and Friedrich Engels (1820-1895), the founders of communist theory.

To briefly sum up, communists in the 19th century (when Marx and Engels were writing) believed society would evolve from its present capitalist form to communism. According to Marxist theory, communism would occur naturally, as it was a political evolution of human society. When it did, economic classes would disappear, as would private property and ownership of the means of production (factories, mines, etc.) When pure communism was attained, all people would be equal in a workers' state. Marx and Engels believed the movement toward communism would first take place in Western Europe, which had industrialized first and seen the greatest societal disruption. Neither Marx nor Engels spoke much about agricultural peasants, which made up most of the population of the Soviet Union and many of the nations of Eastern Europe.

For many in Russia and elsewhere, the Industrial Revolution only made ancient inequalities worse. And it wasn't only the old nobility who oppressed those at the bottom. It was also the growing middle class, which consisted of industrial owners, as they were eager to set themselves up in the trappings of the aristocracy (mansions, furs, jewels, etc.) by exploiting the labor of the working classes.

So, for Lenin and his comrades, communism wasn't something they could wait for. To them, the working classes (including the peasant class in the vast Russian countryside) had suffered enough, and rather than wait on history to guide them into communism, they would take history by the hand and lead it into a system of government in which there were no upper or lower classes—just workers in a workers' state.

Lenin and his compatriots, which included such men as Leon Trotsky (who organized the Red Army) and Josef Stalin, then set about radically changing society in what they called the Union of Soviet Socialist Republics (the USSR).

Within a short period of time, they confiscated virtually all private property, especially the larger businesses and factories in the cities. Much of the larger landholdings in the countryside were seized as well. Many of those in the upper classes who had not fled during the Russian Civil War did so now. Many thousands who did not were imprisoned or executed for being "enemies of the people." Those who were "lucky" simply had their property seized and lived under suspicion as "class enemies" for most of their lives.

Such a radical change did not come without consequence. Though industrial output grew at first, it soon stalled. Farmers hid their crops rather than sell them at controlled prices. People went hungry and began to complain. In some cases, such as among the soldiers and sailors at the base at Kronstadt in March 1921, rebellions occurred. As a result, Lenin backpedaled a bit and began his New Economic Policy (NEP), which allowed private owners of small businesses and farmers to sell their remaining crops (some had to be given to the state) at market prices. Lenin meant for this to be a temporary solution until a more organized and socialistic one could be developed.

The NEP caused a split within the Communist Party, with some believing it to be helpful and others believing it to be a betrayal of true communism. The question was solved with the Lenin's death in 1924, who passed away after a series of strokes.

In Lenin's will, he specifically said that Stalin should be removed from his high position in the Communist Party. Lenin viewed him as too coarse, calculating, and brutal. Though not highly thrilled with Trotsky either, Lenin preferred him over Stalin. However, Stalin managed to alter Lenin's will, making it seem as if he was Lenin's first choice. When the truth came out sometime after Lenin's death, it was already too late. Stalin had occupied some of the lesser-known but more important positions within the country and in the Communist Party, and he put his own men in charge of the police, security, and other departments throughout the nation.

By 1929, Stalin had won his war for power over Trotsky and his allies. Trotsky fled the country (only to be assassinated on Stalin's orders in 1940), and his allies either swore allegiance to Stalin or were, in the dreadful parlance of the time, "liquidated"—killed.

Although Stalin was the main power within the Soviet Union by the early 1930s, he still had rivals. Some of them were Old Bolsheviks, those who had taken part in the Russian Revolution and been friends with Lenin. Among these men were Nikolai Bukharin, Lev Kamenev, and Grigori Zinoviev. Other powerful figures were younger men who had come up after the revolution, the most notable of which was Sergei Kirov (whom the famous Kirov Ballet is named after).

In 1934, Stalin, jealous of Kirov's popularity and growing power, had him assassinated. Of course, the assassination was made to look like the work of a disgruntled former party member, who was said to have blamed Kirov for his failures. The death of Kirov, which Stalin organized via his secret police and for whom he was a seemingly shocked pallbearer, gave Stalin the chance to solidify his power.

In 1934, the first "Great Purge" began, in which hundreds of thousands of people were arrested for being "enemies of the people." Thousands more were executed for either being linked to Stalin's rivals or being in opposition to his plans and government policies.

The purge of 1934 cemented Stalin's place at the top, but most of those arrested, sent to the Gulag (Stalin's notorious system of labor camps), or killed were mostly lower-level functionaries, with some exceptions like Kirov. In 1937, Stalin officially began what is known to history as the Great Purge or the Great Terror.

In 1937, Bukharin, Kamenev, and Zinoviev were put on trial. These were publicized show trials in which all three openly admitted that not only were they working against Stalin, but they had also been agents of capitalism and/or plotters with Trotsky for almost their entire lives. These men were threatened with the deaths of their families, and they were beaten and psychologically tortured behind the scenes. In front of the camera and radio microphones in the court, they admitted their "guilt." All three were convicted and executed.

Also caught up in Stalin's power grab and paranoia was Marshal Mikhail Tukhachevsky, a military hero of the Russian Revolution and Russian Civil War. He had the strength (forces within the Red Army) and the popularity to be a real threat to Stalin. No evidence has ever linked Tukhachevsky to any plot against Stalin, but at his "trial" in 1937, he admitted to plotting capitalist governments to overthrow Stalin. He, too, was executed.

This leads us to events that were to have dire consequences on the Soviet Union's preparedness and abilities when Hitler invaded in 1941. While Stalin was eliminating his political enemies, he began to purge the armed forces' leadership, removing virtually all of the high command of the Red Army (also known as the Stavka).

Out of 80,000 officers in the Red Army, some 35,000 fell victim to Stalin. Many of them were killed. Others were sent to the Gulag, where many more died. The lucky ones "retired" and lived in exile. And this wasn't confined to just the lower officer ranks. Three of the five marshals of the Soviet Union (the highest-ranking officers in the country) were killed. All 11 of the deputies to the Commissar for War, 75 of 85 corps commanders, 110 of the 195 divisional commanders, and all of the flag ranks of the navy were killed. Officers were also punished. Sometimes they were shot, sometimes imprisoned, and sometimes forcibly retired.

As a result of the Great Purge of 1937, Stalin held complete military and political power. No one was willing to take the initiative within the armed forces since it might displease Stalin. No one wanted to "stand out"; an old Russian adage says, "The nail which stands out always gets hammered down." This means that when war came, the Red Army was paralyzed, both literally and psychologically.

Chapter 2 – Stalinism

In 1933, Adolf Hitler came to power, and within a short time, he began to roll back the terms of the Treaty of Versailles, which ended World War I. This treaty put limits on the strength of the German armed forces. At first, this effort was secretive. Strangely enough, the nation that helped Hitler hide his efforts (especially in the area of aircraft development and pilot training) was the Soviet Union.

In return for German expertise in other areas (such as manufacturing and fine tool making), the Soviets opened secret air bases to the Germans and sold massive amounts of agricultural products to Hitler. Their ideological differences were overlooked for the moment, but it put Nazism and communism on a collision course.

In 1935, Hitler announced that Germany would reintroduce conscription and enlarge the army to 500,000 men from the Versailles-limited 100,000. While there were people in the West who were alarmed at Germany's rearmament (most notably Winston Churchill), many people had come to believe that the Treaty of Versailles had been too harsh on Germany. Some also believed that the financial terms placed on Germany were a contributor to the Great Depression.

Another reason many in Western Europe and the United States turned a somewhat blind eye to Hitler's rearmament program was that they believed Germany could be used as a bulwark against the Soviet Union. After all, in Hitler's speeches and in his book *Mein Kampf*, he rails against communism repeatedly and calls for Germany to gain *Lebensraum* ("living space") in the vast plains of the western Soviet Union.

During the 1930s, Stalin went to elaborate lengths to make the world believe the Soviet Union was indeed the "worker's paradise" the communists aimed for it to be. The Communist International, or Comintern, was an organization of communists from countries around the world that was commanded by Moscow. They had agents in Western Europe, America, and elsewhere influencing newspapers and other media to include information about the USSR making unheard-of strides in areas such as industry, agriculture, and equal rights. Soviet propaganda, both at home and for foreign audiences, showed happy workers delivering tons of coal, creating hydro-electric dams, having the latest consumer goods, and being on the cutting-edge of aviation (which, at the time, represented modernity).

The truth was somewhere in between. Journalists and diplomats in the Soviet Union were restricted to Moscow and the bigger cities, such as Leningrad. When they were taken out into the countryside, it was on carefully managed tours of the new collective farms—farms, which were run by tightly controlled soviets ("councils") and which had both abolished private property and increased production greatly.

In various large projects (especially dams, power plants, and bridges), foreigners saw the Soviets advancing by leaps and bounds. This was true to a large degree, though any improvement on what had existed under the tsars would've been thought "miraculous." For all its size and resources, Russia was a poor country in the years after the Russian Revolution.

New housing blocks were built in the cities, which included fancy Western-style hotels that foreigners used when they came to visit (they were *always* under surveillance by the secret police). It seemed as if the populations of the cities were living, or on their way toward living, lives much like those in Western Europe, except without the issues of "class" and prejudice.

However, in many of those housing blocks, workers lived in crowded conditions and had virtually no privacy. The secret police (at that time known as the NKVD) were everywhere and had informants in every building and in all the workplaces. Neighbors ratted out neighbors for anything, whether it was real or made up, to get revenge for some slight or to gain a promotion. Throughout the 1930s (especially from the years 1936 to 1938), people were taken away in the middle of the night in black cars that had their windows painted over (some called them "the ravens" for the carrion-eating bird). They were often never seen again.

Their destination was most often the Gulag—that is if they survived the interrogation, which always asked for "names." They wanted the names of people who denigrated Stalin, other high officials, the system, and the revolution. They wanted those who complained about shortages, work, and living conditions.

One story out of millions will convey the reality of living in Stalin's Soviet Union. Victor Herman, an American of Russian descent, traveled with his father, mother, and sister, along with a contingent of Ford workers, to train Soviets at a new auto plant in the USSR in 1931. Victor's father, a socialist, had fled Russia before the revolution and was eager to return to what he believed was now a "worker's paradise." He applied for Soviet citizenship for his whole family, unbeknownst to his son, who would have objected. Victor was a natural athlete and eventually set the world record for the highest parachute jump in 1934. When asked to signed a paper to authenticate his record, he noticed his citizenship was "Soviet," and he refused to sign. Soon, he was on his way to prison, and then found his way to the Gulag (for *Glavnoe Upravlenie Lagerei*, or "Main Camp Administration"). The Gulag was Stalin's system of labor/concentration camps strung out by the hundreds across the USSR, although they were mainly in the cold of Siberia. Victor's existence was a nightmare of torture, starvation, and being surrounded by death. In his travels, he met a man who had been arrested because his neighbor had overheard him talking in his sleep against Stalin. He had literally been arrested for having an anti-Stalin dream. Victor Herman never gave up his dream of returning to the United States, which he finally did in 1977.

The Gulag provided millions of workers for projects throughout the Soviet Union, mostly in mines, lumber forests, and dam building. Safety was not an issue unless it really impacted production. The prisoners were there to work and to die. No one knows the exact total of deaths and executions that happened in the Gulag and Stalin's prisons, but even the lowest estimates have it in the millions.

The foreigners were shown what Stalin wanted them to see. When they visited a collective farm, they would see happy workers and bountiful crops. Some of those were real, as the government poured inordinate amounts of resources into making them appear successful, but this was not sustainable for the entire nation. Many times, crops would be brought in from other farms and loaded onto trucks and sorting tables for guests to see. Workers were told to smile and be "happy," although they didn't need to be told as they knew what awaited them if they didn't.

The movement toward collective farming was not easy. For one, they were almost always mismanaged by teams of Stalinists who knew nothing about farms. In many parts of the country, farmers, especially "middle-class" farmers, known as *kulaks*, who had been allowed to keep some private property under Lenin, refused to allow their lands and animals to be seized and collectivized. Hundreds of thousands of them were sent to the Gulag. Others were left to beg on the streets. The public was urged to see them as "class enemies," and they were encouraged to ostracize and report them for any small infraction.

Tens of thousands were shot, but not before many of their animals were killed in spite.

The suppression of the *kulaks* and the mismanagement of the collective farms caused a famine to break out in 1932/33, especially in Ukraine. This was partially caused by Stalin, who wanted Ukrainian nationalism crushed, as it was strong in many parts of Ukraine. Stalin also needed to feed his cities, and so what crops did grow were taken to Moscow and other cities. This ensured two things: the cities would not go hungry and revolt, and the foreigners would see food on the shelves.

Making matters worse, Soviet grain collectors were responsible for collecting quotas of grain based on the old records. They would go to an area and gather every last seed and grain. However, even after doing this, the grain collectors still would not have enough. So, they fudged their numbers. This happened up and down the line, as no one wanted to report bad news to the top. As a result, Stalin took the grain for the major cities, often believing there was enough food to go around. When reports came in stating there wasn't enough food, that author would take a one-way trip to Siberia. The famine, which took mainly place in Ukraine and in other areas such as Kazakhstan, resulted in millions of deaths. Estimates run between three and twelve million, with the real number likely near five million.

Illustration 1: Dead and dying people in Kharkiv (Kharkov), Ukraine, 1933 (By Alexander Wienerberger - Diocesan Archive of Vienna (Diözesanarchiv Wien)/BA Innitzer, Public Domain, https://commons.wikimedia.org/w/index.php?curid=3120021).

Still, despite these horrors, by the end of the 1930s, the Soviet Union had grown richer and more powerful. Factories had popped up everywhere (most of them in the west of the country where most of the population lived and which was most at risk from invasion). Hydro-electric dams and power plants spread electricity to parts of the nation that had never had it before, allowing work to go on beyond sundown. And by the end of the 1930s, the USSR was self-sufficient in foodstuffs, though barely. For many people, life had indeed gotten better. As long as you kept your head down and didn't complain, you'd be okay.

The drive to radically change the face of the nation meant that throughout the late 1920s and early 1930s, the growth and development of the Red Army were put on the relative back-burner. Until the late 1930s, Stalin faced no realistic foreign threat to his rule. The Red Army was large enough to maintain order and put down any insurrections, and while its generals planned massive offensives in case of war, the risk to the USSR was minimal during the world's recovery from WWI and the Great Depression.

The Soviets had always spent a large percentage of their annual budget on the armed forces. The Russian Civil War and the military intervention by Great Britain, France, and the United States in the area near Murmansk (undertaken ostensibly to support the Whites; nothing really came from this operation other than casualties and the everlasting suspicion of every Soviet leader until Mikhail Gorbachev) made the Soviets believe that only a well-armed state would prevent their system from falling to the capitalists. Obviously, this suspicion went both ways, but the anti-Soviet propaganda in the West only increased their wariness toward the communist country.

In the table below, you can see Soviet expenditure on the armed forces as a percentage of their budget. The years 1926 and 1929 through 1932, which was the height of the Depression, are not included here, as the data available is only partial and sporadic. Neither is the data for 1939, the year WWII began.

1922	1923	1924	1925	1927	1928	1933	1934	1935	1936	1937	1938
15.6	14.5	12.3	3.4	9.1	11.1	16.1	16.5	18.7	25.6	32.6	43.4

By contrast, in 2019, the figures for the US, China, and Russia are 3.4 percent, 2.0 percent, and 3.9 percent, respectively. You can see that the Soviet Union was spending extraordinary amounts of money on arms in the years before the war. You most likely noticed when the amount began to increase: 1933—the year Hitler came to power.

Chapter 3 – 1938 and 1939

As you may know, by 1938, Hitler was ready to put his plans for the domination of Europe into action. He had already remilitarized the Rhineland (an area of Germany that had been ordered by the Allies at the end of WWI to be free of German troops). He had won a special election in 1935 and restored the Saarland (one of the nation's leading coal-producing areas, which had been under Allied control since the end of WWI) to Germany.

When the Allies did not stand up to him as he moved his forces into the Rhineland (and German forces were under orders to retreat if they did so), Hitler was even more certain that France and Great Britain would not risk another war unless they were attacked directly. World War I and the Great Depression had made them timid.

In Moscow, Stalin saw Hitler's plan unfolding, and he noted the lack of Western response.

In the spring of 1938, after years of machinations by Austrian Nazis under orders from Berlin, Germany annexed Austria, something politicians in the West had said they would do anything to prevent. They did nothing except condemn the move "in the strongest language," as diplomats put it.

Next on Hitler's list was an area of the new nation of Czechoslovakia, which had been formed in 1918 after the dissolution of the Austro-Hungarian Empire after WWI. In the north and west of the country lived a sizable ethnic German population known as the Sudeten Germans. Though there was some prejudice directed against these people by the Czechs, Hitler greatly exaggerated the problems and threatened to invade the area if they were not resolved. Over a period of months, Hitler and the Sudeten Nazis did everything in their power to make the situation worse, not better. Nazi troops massed on the border. The British and French were alarmed, and their politicians had many opinions about what to do, which is exactly what Hitler hoped for. The more opinions, the less likely something would happen.

The Czechs and Slovaks are Slavic people, as are the Russians and many others in Eastern Europe. Historically, Russia was seen by the smaller Slavic nations as sort of a "big brother" they could lean on when times were hard. It was a position that the tsars and even Stalin relished, as it gave them greater influence in Europe. Stalin made it clear to the British and French that if they guaranteed to attack Germany when Hitler invaded Czechoslovakia, Russia would also go to war with Germany. In hindsight, which is always 20/20, this would have likely stopped Hitler in his tracks.

However, with memories of the carnage of WWI still in their minds and the Great Depression not yet over, the Western Allies sought to "appease" Hitler. British Prime Minister Neville Chamberlain and French Premier Édouard Daladier flew to Munich. Hitler was joined by his fascist ally, Benito Mussolini, the leader of Italy. Stalin was left on the sidelines. Not a single Czechoslovakian attended the Munich Conference, which took place from September 29th to September 30th, 1938.

After a series of hurried talks, it was decided the Czechs must give up the Sudetenland to Hitler. The Czechs' army was only strong enough to hold off Hitler if Allied help came. Since it wasn't, the

Czechs were left alone and betrayed. Knowing it was a lost cause, they gave in to Hitler's demands and moved their troops out of the Sudetenland. In March of 1939, Hitler moved his troops into the rest of Czechoslovakia. No one lifted a finger to help.

Neville Chamberlain went home and declared he had achieved "peace in our time." Winston Churchill, on the other hand, condemned the Munich Agreement as a defeat. Hitler told Mussolini, "We have met our enemy and they are worms." Stalin realized he could not count on Britain and France at all, so he determined to come to an arrangement with Hitler.

With increasing intensity through the rest of 1938 and into 1939, Hitler began complaining that the sizable German minority in Poland, especially in the "Free City" of Danzig (today's Gdansk, Poland), was being mistreated and deprived of their rights.

Poland, like Czechoslovakia, came into existence after WWI. Within the country's borders, especially in the west, was a minority German population. Additionally, at the end of WWI, the Allies determined that the German state of East Prussia would be separated from the rest of Germany by a strip of land that became known as the "Polish Corridor." This was done to give Poland access to the Baltic Sea. In truth, it was a peculiar situation, as Prussia was like an island, separated from its homeland.

Hitler called for the elimination of the Polish Corridor and better treatment of Germans within Poland. If things didn't change, he would invade Poland. By this time, the United Kingdom and France had realized the grievous error they had made in Czechoslovakia, and they promised Poland that if Hitler invaded, they would go to war with Germany.

Hitler did not totally discount this, but he believed that if he could defeat Poland quickly, he would be able to shift enough troops to the west to prevent the British and French from taking any meaningful action. Hitler's big worry was the Soviet Union.

Though Poland had been recently restored in 1919 due to the Treaty of Versailles, it had an ancient history. For a time in the late Middle Ages, Poland had been a world power. The Poles were fiercely independent and were the sworn enemies of both Germany and Russia, two of the three countries (the other being Austria-Hungary) that had conquered Poland. Altogether, these three countries ruled over Poland for a combined two centuries, beginning in the early 1700s. Although the Poles welcomed the British and French guarantees of assistance, they would have likely fought Hitler without them.

Poland's eastern border was Russia's western border. Though not a friend to the Poles, Stalin would have much rather had a weak Poland on his border than a strong Germany. Having already seen the lack of willpower of the British and French in the Czech crisis, Stalin made a surprise and secret overture to Hitler.

On August 23rd, 1939, the Soviet and Nazi governments announced to a shocked world that they had just signed a ten-year non-aggression pact. With this move, everyone knew Hitler had just been given a free hand to deal with Poland, as he did not have to worry about Soviet interference.

Of course, there was much more to the Nazi-Soviet Pact (sometimes referred to as the Molotov-Ribbentrop Pact for the USSR's and Germany's foreign ministers, respectively). Within the agreement were secret protocols. In these secret agreements, Stalin and Hitler agreed to split Poland between them. Additionally, Stalin would not have to worry about German interference if (which was more like when) he invaded the Baltic states of Lithuania, Latvia, and Estonia. These were new nations created after WWI that were formerly a part of the Russian Empire. Bessarabia and two other regions of Romania would go to Stalin. Hitler wanted much of Poland and Warsaw, and to do that, he agreed not to interfere in any designs Stalin had on Finland, which had also been a part of the pre-WWI Russian Empire, as well as a former German ally.

Not only were the countries of the world shocked, but communists around the world were too. On August 22nd, they denounced Hitler and the Nazis as the greatest criminals in history. On August 24th, they received directives to cease all anti-Nazi propaganda.

Illustration 2: Contemporary cartoon depicts the Nazi-Soviet Pact as a soon-to-be troubled marriage.

Illustration 3: Using the same names they had called each other for years, Hitler and Stalin greet each other over a fallen Poland.

The Nazi-Soviet Pact also called for the Soviets to send massive amounts of grain, raw materials, and other natural resources to Germany in exchange for German machinery, technical knowledge, and engineers. On the day the Nazis attacked Stalin in 1941, they passed trains heading the other way with grain bound for Berlin.

Hitler invaded Poland on September 1st, 1939. France and Great Britain declared war on Germany two days later. On September 17th, the Red Army invaded eastern Poland, and by September 27th, the Polish government had surrendered. Though the Soviet Union suffered the greatest number of dead during WWII, no nation suffered more than Poland. Nearly 20 percent, which equates to one in five Poles, died during the war. This figure includes the Jewish population that suffered as well, which was an astounding 90 percent.

In June of 1940, Stalin invaded the essentially helpless Baltic states. In all of the areas taken by the Soviets, the same horrible purges and terror that had gripped the USSR in the 1930s began. In the Baltics, Stalin's tactics later drove much of the populace into Hitler's waiting arms, with horrible consequences for everyone. In Poland, terror swept the part of the country under Stalin's control. In just one instance, over 20,000 Polish army officers, politicians, and prominent personalities were executed by the Soviets at Katyn in eastern Poland.

On November 30th, 1939, Stalin attacked Finland. For months, Stalin and his foreign minister, Vyacheslav Molotov, had been demanding that the Finns cede land to the USSR as a buffer against a possible attack by Hitler. They were also worried that the Finns, who were somewhat friendly to Germany, would join Hitler in an attack in the Soviet far north and Leningrad. In fairness, Stalin offered the Finns a larger piece of Soviet territory than what he asked from them, but the territory he offered consisted of much snow and ice, whereas the land he demanded of Finland was strategically valuable.

The Finns refused. The short Winter War that followed was an embarrassment for the Red Army. On the Karelian Isthmus, which stretches north between the Baltic Sea and Lake Ladoga, the Soviets threw waves of ill-prepared and ill-equipped men against strong Finnish defenses. As a result, they were mowed down. To the north, in the pine forests of central Finland, highly trained, motivated, and well-led Finnish ski troops tore apart massive and less mobile Soviet formations.

By March, however, the Soviets had regrouped, replaced many of their leaders (which meant many were shot), and renewed their offensive. The Finns were forced to agree to Stalin's terms. At this point, Stalin was worried about the growing possibility of a German attack, despite his non-aggression pact with Hitler. So, he halted his offensive and made peace with Finland.

The Winter War was an embarrassment for Stalin and the Red Army, despite the improvements implemented at the end of the conflict. Hitler and the rest of the world saw what they believed to be a poorly led and poorly motivated Red Army. Many believe that this was the moment when Hitler decided to attack the USSR when he felt the time was right.

Europe was not the only place where the Red Army was engaged in combat. In the Far East, large Soviet formations (including a large number of tanks) were engaged with Japanese troops along the northern Chinese border and Mongolia along the Khalkhin Gol River from May to September 1939.

To give a brief summary, in 1931, Japan had conquered the semi-autonomous and resource-rich Chinese region of Manchuria. In 1936, the Japanese began an invasion of China itself. The Imperial Japanese Army (IJA) believed that Japan's future lay on the Asian mainland with its wide, open spaces and natural resources (nickel, iron, timber, etc.—at that point in time, the oil resources of the area were relatively unknown). The Imperial Japanese Navy (IJN) knew that oil and rubber were the keys to modern warfare, and they worried more about the forces of Great Britain and the United States in the Pacific than the Chinese or the Soviets. So, the IJN argued for expansion in the Pacific.

By the late 1930s, the Japanese army had gained control of the Japanese government to a large degree, and elements in the IJA in China operated with an amazing degree of arrogant independence. As had happened in China, Japanese troops provoked an incident with Mongolian/Soviet forces, and within a short period, a large-scale battle began.

Stalin sent General Georgy Zhukov (who would later become the preeminent military leader of the Soviet Union's war with Germany) to deal with the Japanese, along with sizable reinforcements. Zhukov was a ruthless commander who paid no real heed to casualties. However, he was also a student of war and had studied the latest books and papers that came out of the militaries of France, Great Britain, and Germany, which all asserted that massed and maneuverable armor would be the greatest factor of the next land war.

The resulting battle was a decisive victory for the Soviets and a humiliation for the Japanese. The Battle of Khalkhin Gol was lodged in Japan's memory so strongly that it was one of the primary factors in its decision to attack across the Pacific and into South Asia in the war to come. But though the Japanese rapidly decided they would not provoke the Soviets again, Stalin and the Red Army leadership remained wary of Japan and left sizable forces in the Soviet Far East rather than deploy them in Europe.

Illustration 4: Vladimir Putin and Mongolian President Khaltmaagiin Battulga view a painting of the Battle of Khalkhin Gol on the eightieth anniversary of the battle in 2019.

Chapter 4 – Interlude

When Stalin agreed to the non-aggression pact with Hitler in August 1939, he was under no illusion the Soviet Union would remain at peace with Germany. Stalin and Hitler had long railed against each other and their respective ideologies. There are various theories as to what Stalin's real beliefs were. At the end of this book, you will find a list of resources that will allow you to examine this question more closely. There are some rather unrealistic theories (such as Ernst Topitsch, who asserts that Stalin's pact with Hitler was part of a well-thought-out "master plan" to cause a devastating war in Europe, with Stalin invading after Europe had bled out). However, most historians agree that the purpose of the pact, at least for Stalin, was to buy time.

The Soviet Union was in a peculiar position when WWII broke out. Its armed forces were huge, but they were poorly led, disorganized, and paralyzed by Stalin's purges in the late 1930s. In 1940, the Soviets began producing two tanks that were better than anything the Germans had in the field at the time (the T-34 and the KV-1). The Soviet air force was gigantic but outdated. Soviet industry was growing by leaps and bounds by the late 1930s, but many people still had barely enough to eat. The Red Army was concerned about Hitler, but it was also faced with millions of Japanese troops in China.

Add to all of that (and more) was Stalin's paranoia. He sometimes believed his intelligence services and spies, but other times, he suspected them of incompetence or even treachery. He had hoped to form an anti-Hitler alliance with France and Great Britain before the Czech crisis of 1938, but he then turned against them in making the pact with Hitler. When intelligence reports from Churchill and others in the West warned Stalin about the forthcoming German invasion, he viewed them with suspicion, believing the "capitalists" wanted him to provoke a war with Hitler so that the West's two enemies, Nazism and communism, would destroy each other.

It's likely Stalin believed a war with Hitler was inevitable—that is, if he wasn't defeated by France and Great Britain, as many believed he might be. Though he was careful not to provoke an incident, Stalin abandoned the line of defenses in the western Soviet Union, known as the Stalin Line, and moved many of his troops into eastern Poland, the Baltics, and the border with Romania (which allied itself with Hitler in the summer of 1940). Arms production increased, as you saw in the table in the prior chapter, more men were drafted, and the number of people in local militias rose.

Still, Stalin was explicit in his orders to his commanders—"do not provoke the Germans." In the weeks before the German invasion in 1941, German reconnaissance planes blatantly crossed into Soviet airspace. Stalin warned his commanders against taking any action against them, and a warning from Stalin was *not* a suggestion.

On April 9th, 1940, Hitler invaded Denmark and Norway. Denmark fell in hours. Norway capitulated after heavy fighting on land and sea.

On May 10th, Hitler launched his invasion of Western Europe, attacking France, Belgium, and Holland simultaneously. The latter two countries fell in days. France fell in an astounding six weeks. The British Expeditionary Force was compelled to retreat back to England from Dunkirk and Calais. Even those who had predicted a German victory were stunned by the speed with which Hitler's forces defeated the Allies.

Stalin was just as shocked, and when France fell, his orders not to provoke the Germans were emphasized.

Aside from the secret protocols that divided Poland and other parts of Eastern Europe, the Nazi-Soviet Pact included very favorable terms for both sides. By the beginning of the Nazi-Soviet war, Hitler would receive nearly one million tons of petroleum, over one and a half million tons of grain, and 140,000 tons of manganese, as well as smaller quantities of other raw materials.

In return, Stalin received technical schematics on the latest German warships, heavy naval guns, a wide variety of machines and machine tools as well, and experts to train Soviet engineers and workers. The pact was surprisingly well balanced, as both nations got what they needed. But as the date of Hitler's planned invasion grew closer (which was originally set for May 15th, 1941), the Germans reneged on large parts of the agreement. Stalin was fully aware of this, yet the trains with Soviet grain and other materials kept flowing westward so as not to provoke Hitler.

The problem was that Hitler did not need a provocation.

Chapter 5 – Barbarossa

For many years, historians and laypeople interested in WWII believed that Hitler's planned offensive, codenamed "Barbarossa" (for the medieval Germanic king Friedrich Barbarossa), was delayed due to Mussolini's abortive invasion of Greece.

This invasion began without Hitler's knowledge in 1940. Mussolini's forces struggled to subdue the Greeks, and Hitler was forced to render aid to the Italians. In order to do so, German forces would have to pass through Yugoslavia, which had been friendly to Germany until March 1941, when a pro-Allied coup toppled regent Prince Paul and placed King Peter II on the throne. With that, Hitler was forced to invade both Yugoslavia *and* Greece. Both of these countries were in German hands in about a month, beginning in April 1940. However, both would become a thorn in Hitler's side throughout the war, particularly Yugoslavia, which drew hundreds of thousands of Nazi troops away from other fronts, particularly in the Soviet Union.

Despite the "side-show" in the Balkans, the real issue (as eminent WWII historian Antony Beevor and others have pointed out) was logistical. The Germans could not get the needed amounts of oil and fuel to the troops preparing to invade the USSR. There was also the problem of massive numbers of French trucks and tanks (many of which were excellent machines) being transferred to the East. It is estimated that when the invasion of the Soviet Union occurred, some 80 percent of their vehicles were French, as the French Army had neglected to destroy them before their surrender in 1940.

Hitler's forces were ready by late June, and on June 22nd, the largest military operation the world had ever seen began. Three and a half million German, Finnish, Romanian, Hungarian, and Italian troops poured across the borders of Poland, the Baltic states, and southern Russia/Ukraine, which was a front stretching some 1,800 miles from north to south. This force included some 6,000 tanks and other armored vehicles, 7,000 artillery pieces, and 7,000 mortars. Anywhere between 3,500 and 5,000 aircraft flew multiple sorties the first day.

Facing the Nazis and their allies were between 2.5 to 2.9 million Soviet troops, who had 11,000 tanks. Most of these vehicles were outdated, though sizable numbers of T-34s, KV-1s, and KV-2s surprised the Germans with their strength, modern design, and firepower. The Soviet air force numbered nearly 11,000 planes, though the vast majority were outdated and obsolete. Over 30,000 artillery pieces were at or near the front. Unfortunately for the Soviets, many of these guns lacked vehicles or horses to move them and proved useless in a highly maneuverable war.

Just hours before the invasion began, a German sergeant with communist sympathies defected to the Soviets, warning them that Hitler was only hours away from attacking. He was roughly treated, and though many on the front lines believed him, the further back he was driven, the more and more he was treated with suspicion and disbelief.

The person in the greatest amount of denial was the one most people would think would be most suspicious of Hitler. Josef Stalin, perhaps the most paranoid and mistrustful man on Earth at the time outside of an asylum, could not wrap his mind around the fact that he had been played. After the first reports of the German attack reached

Moscow, Stalin entered a mental state, which combined shock, disbelief, and depression, for hours.

Stalin had been warned of Hitler's plans by a number of sources. His military at the front sent reports of massive German troop movements. Diplomatic and intelligence officials in Europe sent reports to Moscow with grave misgivings. His spies all over Europe and in Japan told him a German invasion was imminent. Even Winston Churchill sent Stalin a cable warning him of Hitler's intentions. All of this was met with disbelief and doubt, as Stalin suspected a capitalist plot was in the works to provoke him into attacking Hitler, weakening both dictators so the "capitalists" could move in. After June 22nd, Stalin began to believe most of his intelligence agents and diplomats, but his confidence in them came gradually.

The people of the Soviet Union were not even told that their nation had been invaded until late in the evening of the 22nd. When the news was broadcast, it was not Stalin but rather Soviet Foreign Minister Molotov who informed them:

> Our entire people must now stand solid and united as never before...The government calls upon you, citizens of the Soviet Union, to rally still more closely around our glorious Bolshevist party, around our Soviet Government, around our great leader and comrade, Stalin. Ours is a righteous cause. The enemy shall be defeated. Victory will be ours.

Stalin retreated from the Kremlin to his dacha (vacation retreat) in the forest. Stalin was known for his rough, vulgar language, and as he left the Kremlin, he was heard saying, "Everything's lost. I give up. Lenin founded our state and we've fucked it up!" He issued vague orders for his forces to attack and then retreated into himself.

The Soviet leadership was so dependent on Stalin that for nearly eight full days, the Red Army was without any real leadership. No one wanted to risk his neck issuing orders in Stalin's place. It was not until June 30th that the other members of the Central Committee of the

Communist Party of the Soviet Union, along with Molotov and members of the military, visited Stalin in his home.

Some believe that Stalin was putting his leadership to the test. Who could he trust? Who might want to issue orders in his stead? Others say Stalin was simply suffering from nervous exhaustion. What we do know is that Stalin was scared—maybe for the first time in years. He later said he believed that Molotov and the others were there to arrest him. That was not the case, for the group told Stalin they believed that running the war effort needed to be handled by one man. The dictator asked them something along the lines of "Who did you have in mind?" Molotov replied, "You, Comrade Stalin." With that, "The Boss," as he was called by many, came back to life.

Almost two weeks after the German invasion, Stalin addressed the people of the Soviet Union in a long speech, evoking the spirit of 1812, when Napoleon was forced to retreat from Moscow, and reciting the history of USSR relations with Hitler. Of course, he painted the Soviet Union in an innocent light. However, "The Boss" did paint a dire picture of Soviet territorial losses in his opening statement, along with a couple of big lies.

> The treacherous military attack by Hitler-Germany on our motherland, which was launched on June 22nd continues. Despite heroic resistance by the Red Army and although the best divisions of the enemy and his best air force units have already been destroyed and have met their end on the battlefields, the enemy continues to advance and throws new troops into battle. Hitler's forces have succeeded in conquering Lithuania, a considerable part of Latvia, the western part of Byelorussia and part of western Ukraine. The Fascist air force expands the range of its bombers and subjects Murmansk, Orsha, Mogilyow, Smolensk, Kiev, Odessa and Sevastopol to bombardments. A serious danger hangs over our motherland...Comrades! Our forces are boundless. The arrogant enemy will soon experience this...All our efforts in

support of our heroic Red Army and our illustrious Red Navy! All efforts by the population for the destruction of the enemy! Forward, for our victory!

In the beginning days of the invasion, the security forces of the NKVD ran amok. Thousands of people were arrested, and many were shot for charges ranging from supposed sabotage to "defeatism." After he was firmly back in power, Stalin had a number of generals shot.

After the Finnish war, Stalin changed the long-standing Red Army structure. Prior to the debacle in Finland, NKVD and other Communist Party officials stood side by side with military officers in command of formations all the way down to the company level. These men needed to be consulted for virtually every military decision to see if it was in line with "Stalinist thought" or the "party line," which were one and the same, and to verify the army's loyalty. It also nearly paralyzed decision-making. When Stalin recalled these political officers, who were mostly untrained, it was a popular decision in the Red Army. Now, Stalin reinstated the order, which made things at the front worse.

Throughout the country, Communist Party workers and propaganda departments went to work mobilizing and organizing the people. Tighter controls were imposed on factories, collective farms, and other institutions. Rallies were held, and volunteers for the army and local militias were organized. Large numbers of men were drafted, and for many, the time between their entry into the army and their death at the front was a matter of days. Training in some areas near the front amounted to days, sometimes hours, and sometimes never took place at all. Much of what the Soviets did was necessary, but over time, the intervention of political officers in military decision-making was counterproductive, and calls for the populace to act as communists rather than patriots were stopped. Stalin's speech stated that the war with Hitler was not a war with the German people, who,

Stalin said, were mostly workers and peasants held down by the Nazis and capitalists.

The calls for "communist solidarity" and "communist zeal" fell on deaf ears. Over a relatively short period of time, Stalin and the Soviet government began to call on the people to remember Russian victories of the past. Although the USSR was made up of many nationalities and ethnic groups, Russians and the closely related White Russians of Belarus were in the majority, and historically, they were the most powerful and dominant. Russian victories against the German Teutonic Knights of the Middle Ages and many other Russian "glories" were emphasized, as can be seen in the poster below:

Illustration 5: The spirits of Russian heroes Alexander Nevsky, Marshal Mikhail Kutuzov, and a Red Army soldier of the Russian Revolution call upon the Red Army to defeat Hitler.

Chapter 6 – War of Extermination

World War II on the Eastern Front, as you can likely infer from the death totals we provided in the introduction, was extraordinarily brutal. Of course, war by its very nature is brutal, but like much in life, there is a continuum. An American WWII fighter pilot that this writer knew survived a mid-air collision over the Siegfried Line in western Germany in 1944. As he was parachuting to the ground, he noticed a large group of villagers gathering below. When he landed, it was clear to him that they would, at the very least, give him a good beating, although it would probably be something worse. Of all things, an SS officer came to his rescue. He was taken to a prisoner-of-war camp, and though being a prisoner was hard, he told me two things, "I'm glad I wasn't in the Pacific and taken prisoner by the Japanese, and I'm glad I wasn't one of the Russian guys I saw on the other side of the wire in the camp."

Of course, the SS was known for its murderous brutality, but the war on the Western Front and in North Africa was lightyears different from the war in the Soviet Union or the Pacific. In those two places, racial/ethnic animus combined with ideology created a backdrop for the worst kind of atrocities.

The first victim of Hitler's attack eastward was Soviet-controlled eastern Poland. The Poles there were under no illusion as to what was in store for them, but when Hitler's troops entered the Soviet Union itself, some Soviets welcomed the invaders. This was especially true in Ukraine, where Ukrainian nationalism was still strong. This was also where Stalin had created or at least exacerbated a famine that killed millions, never mind the Great Terror, which killed hundreds of thousands more.

Though there were Ukrainian collaborators throughout Hitler's time in the region (many thousands worked in the concentration/extermination camps), the majority of people in Ukraine and elsewhere soon realized that Hitler's reign was going to be even worse than Stalin's.

In Stalin's Soviet Union, former upper- and middle-class segments of the population had suffered greatly in the years following the Russian Revolution and collectivization. During the Great Terror, people who were even suspected of a crime were sent to the Gulag without trial, where millions died. But in the years before the war, the USSR, while far from being the paradise Soviet propaganda painted it to be, had settled into a somewhat peaceful routine. In the cities, people received an education and free healthcare. Members of the working classes had the chance to climb the social ladder on a scale never before seen in Russian history. Women had greater rights than before, and in many cases, they were in positions of responsibility in manufacturing and, to a degree, government.

When Hitler invaded, that all changed. People were not judged on their loyalty, but on their race or, as the Nazis liked to say, "blood." Obviously, they specifically targeted the Jewish populace, whose suffering knew no bounds, but the rest of the Soviet Union's Slavic population was destined for starvation and mass killing, among other minority groups. If Hitler had been able to force the Soviet Union into surrender, the German plan for the western part of the USSR was to feed the population enough to keep them alive and wait for those who weren't murdered to die. When this occurred, German "colonists" would move in and claim the land for the Reich.

Within a month or two, many USSR citizens knew what they were up against. Survivors from the front line areas poured into cities like Moscow and Leningrad with tales of German atrocities and destruction. In a way, the Germans were their own worst enemy. If they had treated the population with at least a degree of respect and not mass terror, they might have won millions of converts to fight against Stalin. But obviously, that's not what Nazism was about.

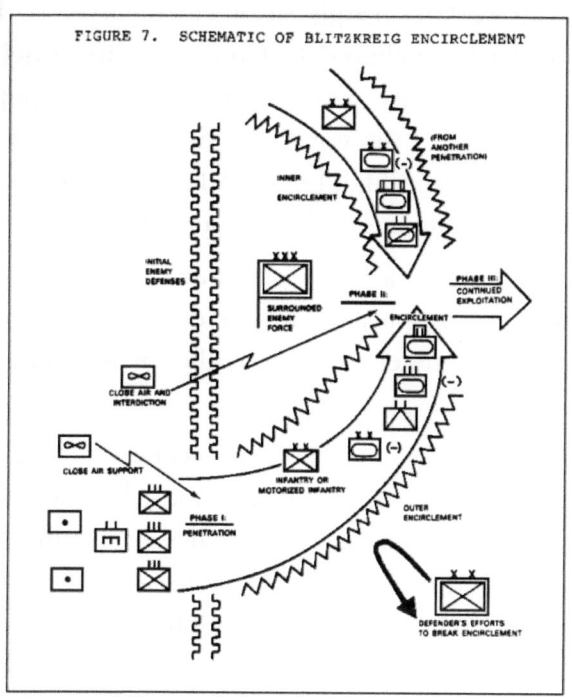

Illustration 6: Blitzkrieg involved the pinning down of enemy units with breakthroughs being exploited by large armored formations, which disrupted the enemy rear and supply lines, to cut off front line troops. This involved a high degree of training, leadership, and coordination.

When the German armed forces attacked, the Soviets knew what was coming, at least as far as the tactics they expected the enemy to use. They had seen it in Poland, Western Europe, and North Africa. However, knowing what an enemy is going to do is one thing; stopping it is another.

The Soviets' pre-war military doctrine called for large numbers of men and tanks to go on the offensive. Militarily, it was thought the Red Army's overwhelming superiority in men and tanks would wear the enemy down. Politically, the Soviet leaders, from Lenin and Trotsky to Stalin, believed that an offensive strategy would show the people the "dynamism" of communism. Soviet troops would also be welcomed by the working people of other countries as "liberators." Secretly, the leadership believed that preparing for a defensive war would be counterproductive and encourage a restive population to rebel. In the latter half of the war (from summer 1943 to 1945), this was exactly what the Soviets did, but in 1941, a combination of factors made the effective execution of this plan impossible.

First, no Soviet general was prepared to take any initiative. Blitzkrieg tactics rely on speed, so a large degree of autonomy had to be given to field commanders. However, after Stalin's purges, that was not going to happen.

Second, even though some units had received training in modern military tactics before the war, the vast majority had not. Zhukov had successfully carried out blitzkrieg-type tactics against the Japanese in Mongolia, but that was on a relatively small scale with trained troops. Zhukov was also given free rein to deal with the Japanese as long as he succeeded, which was not the case in the Nazi-Soviet war. Even troops with training in modern tactics (and this was especially true for armored and air units) did not have the technology needed to carry them out. Tank commanders might have had a radio in their vehicle, but none of the subordinate tanks did, which led to a collapse in communication. This was the same with aircraft, so coordinating tank and air attacks was next to impossible. Flags and hand signals could not be seen in battle, even if tank crews were foolish enough to stand on their turrets to do so, which many of them were.

Third, though Soviet commanders were not prepared to take any real initiative, in the first days and weeks of the war, they received orders to "ATTACK." It's hard to believe, but it almost didn't matter where, how, or with what other units. When orders came in to attack the Germans, that is what they did. It was better to take your chances on the battlefield than disobey orders and be shot in the back by the NKVD.

Fourth, the vast majority of Soviet troops at the beginning of the war had little training whatsoever. Because of the Germans' rapid movements, huge numbers of Soviet troops were killed or captured, along with their equipment. The situation was so dire that new draftees were given a uniform (many times without boots—those lucky enough had shoes from home) and told to pick up the weapon of a man who had fallen near them. This is not an exaggeration.

The western Soviet Union has two notable geographic features: vast forests (some the size of US states) and plains extending to the horizon and beyond for hundreds of miles. At the time, many of those forests were truly impenetrable, especially to military vehicles. It was also difficult to coordinate and move large infantry units within them. Most of these forests were bypassed by the Germans to be swept for stragglers later

On the plains, the blitzkrieg played out as it had in other areas of Europe. German infantry attacks, which were supported by artillery, would target Russian formations and hold them in place. Weak points in the line would be scouted, and armor and air attacks would engage in close coordination and in great strength, driving deep behind the main enemy line and then meeting together to surround the enemy. When the Soviets went on the offensive, it moved the Red Army troops out of defensive positions, which played into German hands.

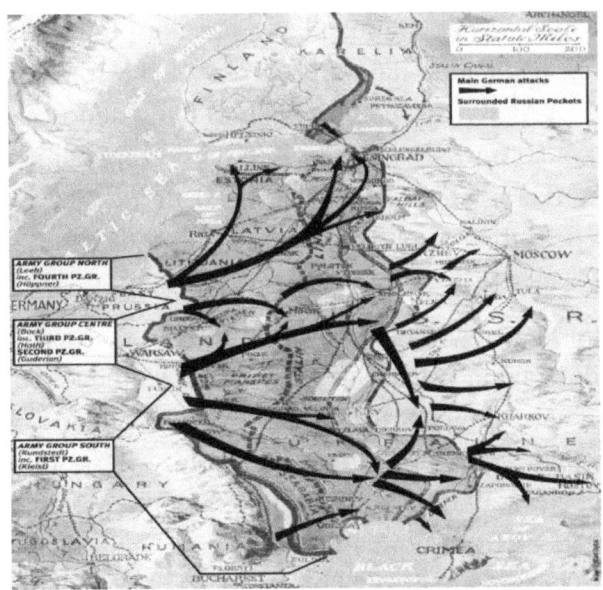

Illustration 7: Operation Barbarossa saw blitzkrieg tactics performed on a massive scale. The pink areas are where hundreds of thousands of Soviet troops were surrounded.

As you can see from the map above, the Soviets were outmaneuvered on a vast scale. German troops and the Nazi leadership all the way up to the Führer believed that it was only a matter of time before the Soviets collapsed completely or begged for terms of surrender.

Heading east, German soldiers and their allies would sometimes wake up in the morning and begin marching in an attempt to catch up with their motorized comrades, walking from sunup to sunset. At times, they would pass hundreds of thousands of Red Army troops heading westward to prisoner-of-war camps.

Illustration 8: Soviet troops marching to an uncertain fate as German prisoners (courtesy US Holocaust Memorial Museum).

Red Army soldiers who were taken prisoner were between a rock and a hard place. More than five million Soviet soldiers died of starvation, disease, or overwork in German concentration camps. Many were shot outright. The first victims of Zyklon-B gas, also known as hydrogen cyanide, were Red Army soldiers at Auschwitz who were used as guinea pigs.

Soviet soldiers who managed to escape were often sent to the Gulag as traitors for being captured in the first place or as suspected Nazi spies. On many occasions, the families of prisoners of war fell under suspicion and/or lost their jobs. At the end of the war, those who had survived German captivity and returned to the USSR were sent directly to the Gulag as traitors or for "re-education." Many did not survive. The war on the Eastern Front was terrible in more ways than most can imagine.

Of course, German soldiers falling into Soviet hands suffered a similar fate. Just as many were shot as were taken prisoner. Those who survived their initial capture were usually sent to the Gulag, where most died. At the beginning of 1943, when the Battle of

Stalingrad ended in a Soviet victory, 91,000 German and allied soldiers were taken prisoner. Only 5,000 returned home.

Though the Soviets fought hard in places (as the Germans moved farther into the USSR, the Soviet resistance did stiffen considerably), the Nazis took chunks of the country at a time. Areas many times the size of the 1938 German Reich fell into Hitler's hands. While the fighting on the front was moving eastward with great rapidity, the Soviets found themselves in another struggle. They needed to save the country's industries, the vast majority of which were in the western part of the nation, and to evacuate as many people from the front line areas (or soon to be front line areas) as they could.

As far as the population was concerned, officials were under Stalin's double-edged sword. If they began evacuating people and factories too soon, they were at risk of being labeled "defeatist" and would possibly suffer serious penalties, including being shot. If they didn't evacuate people and machinery in time, they might be accused of incompetence or, worse, working for the Germans.

After the first few weeks, the situation calmed a bit, as those at the top realized the Germans were moving much faster than anyone had imagined they could. In many cases, the people did not wait to be told to leave by local Communist Party officials; they simply fled in panic as the Nazis approached. However, in many cases, especially away from the main German thrusts (as you can see in Illustration 7 above), huge areas of the country were initially bypassed by the Germans in their attempt to drive deep into the USSR and envelop large Soviet formations. Many towns, villages, and smaller cities were cut off, and they became refuges for fleeing citizens since they were quiet and cut off from communication, at least for the moment. When the front line German troops passed by, reinforcements and occupation troops moved in. Whenever the Nazis arrived, a harsh regime began. Immediately, the Germans moved to arrest any local or regional leaders they could find. Anyone found to be a member of the Communist Party was taken, and in most cases, they were executed.

In some places, particularly the Baltic states (which had been free since 1919 until Stalin annexed them in 1940), massive crowds turned on any remaining Soviets and local communists, often beating them to death.

Unfortunately, anti-Semitism reared its ugly head in the Baltics, as well as in other areas occupied by the Germans. When the Soviets moved into Latvia, Estonia, and Lithuania (especially the latter), many Jews turned to them as relative saviors, heeding their words of a "universal brotherhood of the working classes and equality." Jews in these areas had lived with persecution of various degrees for centuries, and many (but not all) had gravitated toward socialism and communism as a hope for a better future. In some places, Jewish communists were put in positions of power under Stalin's regime. When the Nazis moved in, latent anti-Semitism exploded into the open, which was encouraged by the Germans. Of course, the Germans, in the form of the SS *Einsatzgruppen* ("Special Action Groups"), did most of the killing. Due to the local anti-Semites and the SS, the Baltics were the first nations the SS called *Judenfrei* ("free of Jews"). In other parts of the Soviet Union, especially in western Ukraine, similar things occurred.

In the parts of the USSR that found themselves under German control, the planned exploitation of the populace began, beginning with the food supply, much of which began to flow back to Germany. In some places, the Germans found intact factories, mines, railroads, and other infrastructure. In these cases, the Soviets didn't have time to evacuate or destroy anything while they retreated. In many other towns and cities, infrastructure was destroyed by battles or by shelling and aerial bombings.

However, especially as they marched deeper into the Soviet Union, the Germans found that many of the factories had simply been taken down and removed. Though historians are finding that the number of evacuated Soviet factories and industries was less than originally believed, the Soviet removal and reestablishment of industries farther to the west, which was out of range for German troops and bombers, can be called a modern miracle. Without those industries, it's highly probable the Soviets would have lost the war.

The Soviets moved 2,593 plants out of harm's way. A good chunk, around 1,523 of them, were large plants. Of these major tank, airplane, weapon, and munitions plants, 226 were moved to the Volga region, 667 to the Ural Mountains, 244 to western Siberia, 78 to eastern Siberia, and 308 to Kazakhstan and the other Central Asian Soviet republics. Some of the plants that had been moved to the Volga region were relocated to the Stalingrad area, where many continued production as the battle raged around them. During the German 1942 summer offensive in the southern Soviet Union, more industries had to be moved, including a number that had been evacuated earlier.

As one might expect, this did not go off without a hitch. Sometimes, the workers of these plants ended up hundreds of miles from their equipment. Sometimes equipment was dumped in the middle of nowhere to fulfill quotas and speed requirements only to be found later. In some cases, this was what was instructed, and a considerable number of factories restarted production in the open air, powered by diesel generators.

Some factories got up and running very quickly. Parts of the Leningrad Kirov tank factory were evacuated in early August and were producing tanks again by September 1st in another part of the country. Of about 1,500 plants evacuated during the second half of 1941, about 1,200 were in operation again in 1942.

Soviet production was staggering even though its most productive and populated areas fell to the Germans. Despite that, Stalin constantly demanded more aid from the Western Allies. This aid had begun on a very small scale before the United States became involved in the war, but with the entry of the world's greatest industrial power, the aid to the USSR increased year by year and also included agricultural products.

Though the United States and Great Britain sent weapons to the Soviets, including tanks and fighter planes, the Russians became relatively self-sufficient in those sectors by late 1942. The tanks (which included the US pre-war main battle tank, the M3 Lee, and the later M4 Sherman, which were both inferior to Soviet tanks) and planes (mainly reconnaissance planes and relatively obsolete P-39 Airacobras) were not needed as much as small arms and anti-aircraft guns, transportation, and raw materials, especially rubber. Hundreds of thousands of American trucks and jeeps helped the Soviets greatly in the war effort.

These supplies came over the Iranian border in the south (that country was jointly occupied by the Soviets and the British in 1941 to ensure the supply route), into Central Asia via India, and, most famously, via the Murmansk convoys in the Arctic Circle. These merchant convoys sailed through not only some of the most atrocious weather on Earth but also through heavy concentrations of German U-boats, which sometimes took such a toll on the merchantmen that the convoys had to be halted on occasion.

Illustration 9: The conditions facing the naval and merchant ships of the Murmansk convoys were brutal for much of the year.

As far as the population, evacuations were sometimes well organized and timely, but they often were not. Two of the more tragic examples were at Leningrad in the late summer of 1941 and at Stalingrad in 1942. In both cases, hundreds of thousands of civilians were evacuated, but both cities housed millions of people. During the two-and-a-half-year siege of Leningrad, one million civilians died. At Stalingrad, the number was in the hundreds of thousands. This happened throughout the country on a smaller scale.

It is amazing that despite the loss of most of its most productive and resource-rich areas and the deaths or capture of millions of people, Soviet production increased year by year with the exception of 1945, the war's last year. Below you will see a table for the main categories of Soviet defense production.

	1940	1941	1942	1943	1944	1945
Aircraft	10,565	15,735	25,436	34,845	40,246	20,102
Tanks/self-propelled guns	2,794	6,590	24,446	24,089	28,963	15,419
Artillery/mortars (thousands)	53.8	67.8	356.9	199.5	129.5	64.6
Rifles/carbines (millions, except 1945)	1.46	2.66	4.05	3.44	2.45	574,000

Chapter 7 – The Major Battles

The war on the Eastern Front involved millions of men on both sides from many nationalities, including Russian, German, Finnish, Hungarian, Romanian, Italian, and Spanish, not to mention the many ethnic groups that made up the Soviet Union. Tens of thousands of battles raged from 1941 to 1945, most of them only remembered by historians who specialized in the subject and the veterans of the battles themselves.

However, a number of battles fought on the Eastern Front were monumental and earth-shattering: the opening invasion of Operation Barbarossa, which the Germans executed with amazing speed, Leningrad, Moscow, Stalingrad, Kursk, Operation Bagration, and Berlin.

Barbarossa

Within the opening months of the war, a series of huge battles took place, most of them resulting in tremendous Soviet defeats and losses in manpower. As you read in a prior chapter, the Germans used their blitzkrieg tactics to great effect all along the front, piercing the Soviet front lines and driving deep behind masses of Soviet troops before they could react, cutting them off from reinforcements and supplies.

The Germans surrounded and eliminated hundreds of thousands of Red Army troops at places such as Bialystok, Poland, near Minsk in Byelorussia (present-day Belarus), near Uman and Kiev (often spelled as Kyiv today) in Ukraine, and at Bryansk, Smolensk, and Vyazma on their drive toward Moscow. That is not to say the fighting was easy. The Germans sustained tremendous casualties themselves, and they were less able to sustain them than the Red Army was.

During Operation Barbarossa, which began on June 22nd, 1941, the German death toll approached 200,000 in December 1941, with another 40,000 missing in action and nearly 700,000 wounded. Large numbers of tanks and aircraft were destroyed, nearly 3,000 each. Their allies sustained 150,000 killed, wounded, or missing.

Large as these numbers were, they were dwarfed by the losses inflicted on the Red Army. Almost 600,000 Soviet soldiers were killed, nearly 300,000 died from disease, hunger, cold, or execution (the Soviets executed soldiers for desertion, and the Germans were also responsible for atrocities committed against the Soviets on or near the battlefield). Nearly one and a half million men were wounded, and three million Soviet soldiers were captured (about one-quarter of these were reservists who were captured before they could enter battle). Soviet losses in tanks and aircraft were astounding: over 20,000 each. A majority of the Soviet airplanes were destroyed on the ground in the opening days of the war.

If the Soviets outnumbered the Germans so greatly in men and materiel, how and why did the Germans win battle after battle in the war's opening months? Some of the reasons have already been discussed: Stalin's depression and orders to simply attack, which played right into German hands; lack of initiative on the Soviets' part combined with lack of experience in both command and in the field; and highly experienced German officers and troops with exceedingly high morale and a proven, well-tested battlefield theory that was executed almost flawlessly.

Still, beginning around late August/early September 1941, from Hitler down to the lowest German soldier in the field, the Nazis began to scratch their heads and ask themselves a series of questions: "How can the Reds keep fighting?" "Where are all these men coming from?" "Why did no one know that most of the Soviet tanks were better than ours?" As the Germans got closer to the capital of Moscow and the USSR's "second city," Leningrad, they also saw a stiffening of Soviet resolve. Though large numbers of Soviet troops were still surrendering, those numbers were growing smaller, as the Soviet soldiers were fighting harder and more skillfully.

Also taking a toll on German morale were the vast expanses of the USSR. Germany is a small country, about the size of the US states of Washington and Oregon combined. Many Germans at that time had never been outside of their home state or region, and now, they were confronted with mile after mile of unlimited plains with virtually no landmarks.

In the summer, Germany was hot and dusty. Starting in late September/early October, it began to rain. Russia has two rainy seasons: fall and spring. In each case, especially in the war years and before paved roads became common in the country, the rain turned everything into swampy mud. Russians have a name for the rainy season: *Rasputitsa*, meaning "The Sea of Mud" or "The Time of Mud." It bogged down tanks and horses, which powered the German army to a larger degree than motor transport, slowing the German advance on Moscow.

Illustration 10: German troops pulling a command car through the Russian mud. The Nazi flag is on the hood of the car to identify it to German planes to avoid friendly fire (courtesy Bundesarchiv).

By the end of October, the Germans were worn out by the mud and rain, the increasingly fierce Soviet resistance, and logistical problems, which included the breakdown of many of their tanks and vehicles and the lack of replacement parts. Even Hitler realized the likelihood of his men taking Moscow in 1941 was slim to none, but he determined to drive on before the winter set in.

However, knowing what the Russian winter is like from reading about it in a book or an intelligence report is far different from experiencing it. The more cognizant German officers and men knew they were ill-prepared for the coming cold weather, but it wasn't until after it had set in that Hitler and the Nazis realized how ill-equipped their troops were. At that point, desperation took root, and Germany set up a nationwide drive to encourage German men and women to donate winter clothing. It was not an unusual sight to see battle-hardened German troops wearing women's fur stoles and minks on the front lines. However, most of what was collected arrived too late to help the troops in front of Moscow.

Illustration 11: Aside from the white-washed helmets, these Germans troops, like most, were ill-prepared for the Russian winter. Note the clothing, which was better suited to fall than -20°F temperatures.

Illustration 12: By contrast, many Soviet troops were better prepared for the weather, especially those brought west from Siberia.

The responsibility for the defense of Moscow was given to General (later Marshal) Georgy Zhukov, with General Ivan Konev, another future Hero of the Soviet Union, as his second-in-command. Zhukov had been responsible for the Soviet victory over the Japanese at Khalkhin Gol and had organized the defense of Leningrad in the fall, preventing the Germans from taking that important city.

Stalin and the Soviet leadership had debated on whether to leave Moscow in October. In the end, it was decided that if they left, Soviet morale might take a fatal hit. So, they elected to stay, coordinating hundreds of thousands of citizens in preparing defenses around the city.

On November 7th, Stalin ordered a military parade to be held in Red Square. To this day, the November 7th parade is remembered for showing the world that the Soviets meant to fight it out. The troops that took part in the parade marched directly to the front.

Despite the difficulties, the Germans attempted one final push on Moscow before the weather made it impossible. On November 15th, they began an offensive to the south of the city, with the aim of driving behind the capital and cutting it off from the rest of the country. They made progress despite the weather and repeated Soviet counterattacks, which were urged by Stalin but frowned on by Zhukov, as they were wasteful in the extreme. At one point, some German troops reported seeing the spires of St. Basil's Cathedral in the Kremlin off in the distance. It was as far as they ever got.

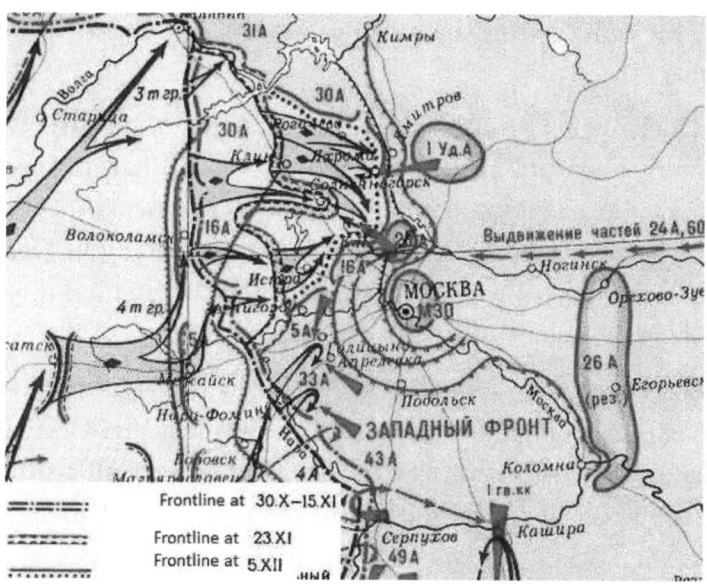

Illustration 13: A map seldom conveys the intensity of a battle, but this one comes close. Above is a Soviet map showing the repeated German drives on Moscow and the rings of Soviet defenses along with Red Army counterattacks up to December 5th, 1941.

In the spring of 1941, Soviet spy Richard Sorge, who was working in Tokyo undercover as a journalist, had warned Stalin of the upcoming German invasion. Stalin did not believe him. In late 1941, information from Sorge and others in Japan reported that Japanese war plans did not include an attack on the USSR. This time, Stalin trusted the information, and he ordered most of his Far Eastern troops westward. Eighteen Soviet divisions, many of them well trained, experienced, and well equipped for winter, moved rapidly westward. Among these eighteen divisions were a number of armored divisions, which totaled 1,700 tanks. One and a half thousand planes also made the trek from one side of the nation to the other.

Hitler's generals and intelligence departments reported that his troops near Moscow were worn out, having been stopped by logistics, weather, and the Soviets. This was true, but they also told the Führer that the Soviets were in the same state. Accordingly, Hitler was more concerned with his plans for the spring and other fronts when the Red

Army gave him a truly unwelcome surprise in the first week of December.

On December 4th, the Soviet 4th Shock Army (the Soviet "Shock" armies were often put in the vanguard of Soviet offensives and given significantly more tanks and artillery than other Soviet armies) and the 20th Army attacked the Germans north of the capital. On December 6th, the 10th Soviet Army attacked south of the city. Behind them were hundreds of thousands of Red Army soldiers.

In total, the Soviet counterattack included over one million men, and though this completely surprised the Germans, the Germans had a similar number of troops in the area. However, offensive forces choose the point of attack and the forces that are sent there, and in this case, the Soviets overwhelmed many German defenses with sheer numbers. Additionally, they were well rested and better equipped for winter, and for the first time, they had truly sizable quantities of the new T-34 tank at their disposal,

The T-34 is often called the "best all-around tank of WWII." While some German tanks later in the war, such as the Panther and Tiger, were qualitatively better in many respects, they also had serious flaws that the T-34 did not. For instance, the Panthers and Tigers were overengineered and took too long to produce, and spare parts were intricate and difficult to manufacture. Both German tanks, especially at first, were subject to mechanical breakdown. By contrast, the T-34 was easy and quick to build, reliable, easy to operate, and powerful enough to challenge most German tanks, especially with the numbers on their side.

The Germans were driven back between 90 to 250 miles in different places before reinforcements arrived from other fronts, allowing their defenses to stiffen. The Soviet Moscow offensive, while not a strategic turning point like Stalingrad would be the next year, showed the Germans, the Western Allies, and the Soviet people that the Red Army had the capacity to defeat the Nazis on the battlefield, something they had not been able to do effectively until then.

Making things even worse for the Germans, Hitler decided to honor his alliance with Japan, and he declared war on the United States of America on December 11th, just days after the Japanese attack on Pearl Harbor.

Leningrad

Leningrad (today's St. Petersburg) was the USSR's "second city" and had been the capital of the Russian Empire from 1732 to 1918, after which Moscow was named as the capital again. Leningrad was the home of the Bolshevik Revolution and was known as the center of culture and fine arts in Russia. It is one of the most beautiful cities in the world, and it is often called the "Venice of the North" for its many canals. Hitler had a special hatred for Leningrad for all of these reasons, and he decided not only would the city be one of the prime targets for his invasion, but it would also be wiped off the face of the earth and the land given to his allies, the Finns.

German Army Group North was responsible for the attack on Leningrad, and it had been making its way steadily toward the city since the invasion of the USSR began, driving through northern Poland and the Baltic nations to do so. To Hitler's dismay, the Finns refused to join the attack on the city, which might have cost Hitler his victory there. The Finns had told Hitler they would only make war on the Soviets to get back the land that had been taken from them by Stalin in the Winter War of 1939/40. Since Finland had never included Leningrad, they refused to help, staying true to their word.

By September 15th, the Germans had cut the city off from the rest of the country. German shells had already begun falling on the city on September 4th. Leningrad was a city of nearly three million people when the war began, and the prior German attacks had driven refugees from the surrounding country into the city, making a bad situation worse. Four hundred thousand civilians were evacuated from the area before the Germans arrived, but that still left millions trapped.

The Germans began bombing the city shortly after Operation Barbarossa began, but in mid-September, they began sending hundreds of bombers at a time. On the 23rd, hundreds of German bombers destroyed most of the city's food warehouses, as well as seriously damaging hospitals and other vital institutions. This would only add to the tragedy to come.

Though the Soviets began to construct anti-tank and anti-aircraft defenses around the city in the late summer, they had neglected to store enough food. Making matters worse was the reluctance of Soviet officials to report bad news to Stalin. As a result, the Soviet High Command was unaware of the shortfall in food, a problem that was only compounded by the destruction of the food warehouses. When the Germans surrounded the city, Leningrad only had enough food supplies to last for a few weeks. Fuel supplies were also limited, and the main electrical plants were not only damaged by the German bombings but also needed oil for their generators.

Leningrad needed some 600 tons of food a day, and barely any food got into the city after the Germans surrounded it. The only route open to the Soviets was across Lake Ladoga on the northern side of the Karelian Isthmus. When the siege of the city began, only a small number of boats were available. These had to brave intense German air attacks. The only hope for the city was the lake freezing over, which would allow the Red Army to bring supplies across the ice. This eventually happened, but not before hundreds of thousands of people starved to death. In actuality, the death toll in Leningrad was over a million. The siege is often called "the 900 Days," although it stopped just short of that.

The first winter of the siege was the worst, but people continued dying until the German ring was broken in late January 1944. The food ration dropped as low as 125 grams of bread a day for an adult. Workers and soldiers got a little more, but it was still not enough. Within weeks, all of the dogs and cats in Leningrad were killed and eaten. Tree bark and leather were boiled to make "soup." Sawdust and other virtually inedible ingredients were added to the "bread" to stretch the supply. Anything wooden was burned for heat; at times, the temperature fell as low as -40°F for extended periods.

Worst of all, as the winter of 1941 wore on, cannibalism was reported. This was denied for years by the Soviet authorities, but it was proven conclusively by American writer and Russian expert Harrison Salisbury in the early 1970s. When the USSR fell in 1991, records that were finally opened to the public bore out many instances of cannibalism in Leningrad. Most of the incidents involved people devouring those who were already dead, but there was also a larger-than-imagined number of instances of people being killed at night and later sold on the black market as "pork" or "meat pies." People caught eating a corpse were given lengthy prison sentences. Those convicted of killing people for food were shot on the spot—nearly one hundred people were killed for this crime during the siege.

When Lake Ladoga froze, the Soviets slowly began to bring trucks loaded with supplies over the ice. In that first winter, not nearly enough supplies were brought over, but by the late spring, when the ice started to melt, the amount of food, fuel, and other necessities increased. A number of trucks actually fell through the ice, sometimes taking their crews with them. Despite this, by winter of 1944, the "Ice Road" or "Road of Hope" was bringing in just enough to sustain the city's population. The operation itself was an incredible feat of engineering and determination. A railroad was even built across the ice. Warming stations, hospitals, barracks, anti-aircraft defenses, and more were also constructed on Lake Ladoga, whose ice could be six feet thick in winter.

The military aspects of the siege were rather mundane in the grand scope of the Eastern Front. For two and a half years, the Germans shelled and bombed the city, trying to destroy morale and the city's infrastructure. Before the war, Leningrad produced about 10 percent of the manufactured goods of the USSR. During the war, the factories continued to produce with supplies brought in from the outside, sometimes doing so in buildings without heat or even roofs. Tanks that had been built in the city rolled out onto the battlefield without paint; this was how badly they were needed.

In early 1944, the Germans were being pushed back all along the front by the Red Army, but they tenaciously hung onto their grip around Leningrad until the Soviet Operation Iskra ("Spark") broke the siege.

Stalingrad

The Germans were still immensely strong after their unsuccessful attempt to take Moscow. They held large areas of the western Soviet Union and most of Europe, but they were not the power they had been in June 1941. Hitler had gambled everything on destroying the USSR in just a few weeks or months, and instead of getting weaker, it seemed the Soviets were getting stronger. Assisting the Soviets in this situation was Great Britain and the United States, particularly in the area of raw materials, anti-aircraft guns, medium- and large-caliber machine guns, trucks, and jeeps.

Despite this help, the Soviets were still falling behind. They had sustained great losses in men, materiel, and resources. Their soldiers were still largely lacking the training necessary to defeat the Germans decisively in open battles. However, the Soviet generals were beginning to understand their own mistakes. Those who did not learn ended up dead on the battlefield or, in the case of many higher-ranking officers, in front of a firing squad. Some were sent to areas far from the front when they showed talent in other areas, such as training or logistics. Stalin was a hard-taskmaster, but this was a war for the survival of not only the USSR but also of the people who inhabited it.

1942 turned out to be the crucial year. This was the year that the war slowly turned around for the Soviets, as well as the Western Allies, with an emphasis on "slowly."

In the late winter of 1942, Hitler and his generals began planning their spring offensive. Some of Hitler's generals encouraged him to call a halt to the offensive operations in the Soviet Union and instead build strong defenses, pulling back to better positions to do so if necessary. Of course, even those with limited knowledge of the war and the Führer know this did not happen. Hitler, along with a sizable group of supporters both in the Nazi Party and in the military, believed that victory was still in sight, despite the setbacks near Moscow.

What was clear to even Hitler was that his armies in Russia were nowhere near as strong as they had been, and without considerably weakening his forces elsewhere in Europe, they were likely to stay that way. The number of eligible German men were dwindling to the point where they could not be replaced. As time went on, the age limits for the German military were both decreased and increased, which raised numbers but hardly effectiveness.

Still, the German forces in the USSR were still powerful, and Hitler determined that 1942 would be the year of final victory. Most of his generals and enemies expected that Hitler would order a huge push on Moscow when the weather improved, but Moscow was no longer as important to the Germans as it had been.

Two things were of more importance to Hitler in his planning for 1942: 1) seizing the Soviet oil fields in the Caucasus, along with other resource-rich areas in southern Russia and Ukraine, and 2) cutting off those supplies and resources to the Soviets. To do that, Hitler and his commanders developed *Fall Blau* ("Case Blue").

Case Blue had two components. The first was for the Germans to push southward into the Caucasus, pressing on to capture its rich oil fields, which culminated in the fields at Baku on the peninsula's far southeastern side. The second was to move directly east to the city of Stalingrad on the Volga River, Europe's longest river. Stalingrad was a major industrial center, producing over 10 percent of the USSR's heavy machinery and steel products. In wartime, that meant tanks, along with other weapons. Taking Stalingrad would also cut off the supplies moving northward on the Volga River. Successfully accomplishing either would deal a serious blow to the Soviets, and taking both might end the war.

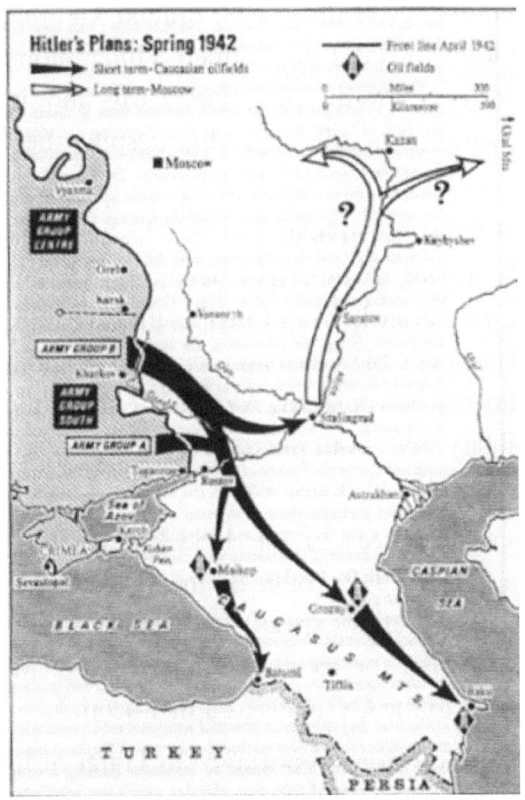

Illustration 11: The tentative German plans for the spring of 1942, including a possible drive behind Moscow if the first stage was successful.

To accomplish this, German Army Group South was divided into two commands: Army Group A and Army Group B.

Army Group A was tasked with taking the Caucasus, and it was the "weaker" of the two groups. It was commanded by Field Marshal Wilhelm List and included the German 1st Panzer Army, 11th Army, 17th Army, and the Romanian 3rd Army.

Army Group B was commanded by General Friedrich Paulus and included the German 4th Panzer Army, 2nd Army, and 6th Army (Hitler's largest). Attached to Army Group B were the Italian 8th

Army, Romanian 4th Army, and the Hungarian 2nd Army. Army Group B was stronger than its counterpart, but it did have a fatal weakness. The Italian, Hungarian, and Romanian armies were poorly equipped and poorly motivated. When the time came, this proved to be crucial.

The German forces amounted to approximately 1.5 million men, nearly 2,000 armored vehicles, and about 2,000 aircraft of various kinds. Soviet forces in the area eventually came to approximately 1.7 million men, between 3,000 and 3,800 tanks, 1,500 to 2,000 aircraft, including combat and non-combat planes, and over 16,000 guns. Another estimated one million were either being trained and in reserve.

Like they had been in June 1941, Stalin and the Stavka were fooled in the spring of 1942. They believed the main German push would be toward Moscow, so they planned accordingly. Many of the forces listed above were initially deployed near the capital and had to be rushed south. The Germans actually conducted a massive deception operation in order to fool the Soviets into thinking Moscow was the target, which included false radio messages, fake troop movements, and "secret plans" that happened to fall into Red Army hands.

Case Blue began in late June after being thrown off its timetable by a poorly planned Soviet offensive that was designed to focus the Germans away from Moscow. The German 6th Army defeated this attack with relative ease and began their own push eastward after resupplying.

The Germans began in stages between June 24th and 28th. As had happened the prior summer, they drove the Soviets back, catching them relatively unaware. Though large numbers of Soviet soldiers were taken prisoner, the Red Army generally retreated in good order, with fewer men surrendering or being cut off than in 1941. Both branches of the German attack moved with great speed in the initial stages of the attack.

The terrain of the Caucasus is very different than the area near Stalingrad. It's more rugged, was less developed at the time, and the very difficult and high Caucasus Mountains divide the region in half. This meant the Soviets could deploy fewer men to the area, as they could count on the terrain and strong defenses near the oil fields to stall or halt the Germans.

Toward the end of August, it became clear to both sides that the battle for Stalingrad was going to be at the center of the German and Soviet war efforts for the foreseeable future. Large battles were fought in the miles leading to the city, especially when the Germans attempted to cross the wide Don River. The Don was the last serious natural obstacle on the way to Stalingrad.

In July, after the Germans cut the main railroad linking Stalingrad and the Caucasus, Stalin took matters into his own hands. He personally wrote the famous Order No. 227, more frequently known as the "Not One Step Back" order. In his own rough language, Stalin decreed that those retreating without orders would be shot or sent to penal battalions and given the roughest assignments, like defusing mines under German fire. Officers who issued retreat orders without authorization would be shot. Behind Soviet front line units, NKVD "blocking units" would be stationed, with orders to kill any men they caught fleeing the battlefield. The order was never disseminated in print. Instead, it was broadcast over the radio and loudspeakers repeatedly for the Red Army to hear. Some say Order No. 227 helped the Soviet defense stiffen. Others, including veterans, said by late 1942, most Soviet soldiers realized exactly how dangerous the situation was and how brutal the Germans were—in other words, they didn't need Stalin to tell them. Regardless, both points of view show how desperate the situation had become.

By the end of September, the German drive in the Caucasus had begun to slow down. It was hampered by the Red Army, the terrain, and the immense distance supplies had to travel to reach them. The oil fields the Germans captured were thoroughly destroyed by the retreating Soviets, and they would likely remain useless for a year or more even if the Germans had succeeded in driving the Soviets back from Stalingrad.

Accordingly, German troops were shifted north to aid in the capture of Stalingrad. For reasons of personal pride and national honor, both sides were determined to take or defend the city named after the Soviet dictator.

On August 23rd, 1942, the *Luftwaffe* (the Nazi air force) launched a massive attack on Stalingrad. Thousands of civilians were killed, and much of the city's center and residential areas were flattened. The key factory areas in the north and south of the city were damaged, but they continued to produce items while the battle raged around them in September.

German troops miles away watched the smoke rise some three miles over the plains and city. Reports from pilots made it seem like Stalingrad had been destroyed, and many Germans believed the city would fall to them rather easily. They could not have been more wrong. For one, the bombing of the city had actually benefited the defenders. The massive amounts of rubble created choke points and "natural" defenses. It wouldn't take long for the Russians to create tunnels and trenches under and through the city, enabling them to spring upon the Germans from behind without being observed.

As the Germans moved into the city, a new Soviet commander took over the Soviet 62nd Army: General (later Marshal) Vasily Chuikov. Chuikov had joined the Red Army as a teenager during the Russian Civil War and had been wounded a number of times. He was also one of the few successful Soviet commanders in Finland and had commanded troops in the Soviet invasion of Poland.

By early November, the Germans were in possession of about 90 percent of the city, but the fighting was beyond tough—it was brutal. One reason is that both sides began to get the feeling that this battle might decide the outcome of the war in Russia and fought accordingly. Another is that Chuikov and his junior officers ordered their men to "hug the enemy." This was done in response to the initial

German superiority in tanks, guns, and planes. By getting close to the enemy, the Soviets hoped to mitigate these German strengths, hoping that the Nazis would not be able to bomb them without hitting their own men. In many cases, this worked beautifully.

Still, by late November, the Soviets were reduced to holding a small area on the Volga River's western bank, which allowed men and supplies to come into the city. This was a very risky Soviet strategy. By early November, they realized two main things: 1) the Germans were tired, sick, and malnourished, and 2) the Nazis kept pouring reinforcements into the city but were neglecting their flanks. The bulk of Axis troops to the north and south of the city were Hungarian, Italian, and Romanian, all of whom were substantially weaker than their German comrades. So, as the Germans kept sending more men into the city to hopefully take it before the bad weather set in (which they were still underprepared for, despite their experience of the prior year), the Soviets pulled back, placing enough men into the foothold on the Volga to hold it.

That isn't to say they "let" the Germans have the city. Fierce and brutal fighting took place in and below the city in the sewers. Snipers hunted officers, radiomen, and each other. Germans and Russians sometimes held parts of the same building, fighting from floor to floor with grenades, knives, shovels, makeshift clubs, pistols, and their bare hands. When the fight for Stalingrad ended, more than one million men (both Axis and Soviet) had been killed or had died from frostbite, sickness, or starvation.

By the beginning of October, the Soviets began the plan for a counterattack. To do this, they would not waste men trying to dislodge the Germans from the city. No, they would attack the weaker flanks, drive deep behind German lines from the north and south of the city, and envelop not only the forces in Stalingrad but also those behind it. Realizing the Germans had placed virtually all their hopes on a victory, the Red Army was able to remove sizable numbers of men from other areas of the front. They did this very secretly, employing some of the same tactics the Germans had before the battle. As the Soviet troops neared the city, they were ordered to move only by night. Security was very, very tight.

On November 19th, the Soviets launched Operation Uranus, which was a massive offensive to the north of the city. On the following day, while the Germans were busy trying to figure out the situation in the north, the Red Army launched its attack in the south.

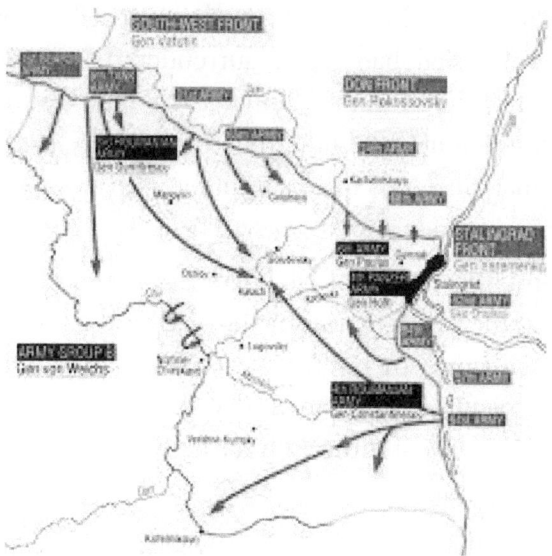

Illustration 12: Operation Uranus. The Soviets attempted to drive even farther west, to the Don River, but were halted. Regardless, they surrounded close to 300,000 German and Axis forces in and around Stalingrad.

By November 22nd, the Soviet pincers had linked up, locking the Germans and their allies in what would become an ever-shrinking pocket. At Hitler's headquarters, panic nearly set in. Debate raged for days over whether the German 6th Army, which was in the city, should be ordered to try to break out to the German lines or if Generals Erich von Manstein and Hermann Hoth should break into the city. They even debated on if both should occur, as it would allow the men in the *Kessel* (the German military term meaning "hedgehog") to retreat west. Days went by. At the beginning of December, Manstein launched a large tank offensive in the southwestern portion of the pocket, and for the first day and a half, he made decent progress, but the -40°F weather, poor German morale, and massive Soviet counterattacks stopped the rescue attempt many miles short of the German line.

The failure of Manstein's rescue attempt meant the men in Stalingrad were doomed. Most of them, including General Paulus (who was named Field Marshal in the hope that he would realize a German Field Marshal had never surrendered his troops or been taken alive), surrendered in late January. Another group in the north of the city surrendered in the first week of February 1943. Ninety-one thousand German and Axis troops went into Soviet captivity, and only five thousand returned home.

For decades, the Battle of Stalingrad was considered to be *the* turning point in the war, not just for the Soviets but also for the Allies. The losses sustained by the Germans at Stalingrad were irreplaceable, and the more cognizant Germans knew this was the beginning of the end. Still, the following summer, Hitler tried one more time to go on the offensive in Russia.

Kursk

The largest tank battle in history began on July 5th, 1943, near the central Soviet city of Kursk in Ukraine. It was the last time the Germans were able to launch an attack of any significance on the Eastern Front. Its codename was Operation Citadel.

Humiliated by the defeat at Stalingrad, Hitler decided to concentrate a huge armored "fist" (as he called it) on both sides of a Soviet bulge in the German lines near Kursk. This would include hundreds of the new Panther and Tiger tanks (the former of which was relatively new and still full of mechanical bugs, mostly in its complicated transmission), along with hundreds of advanced German Mk IV tanks, tank destroyers, and self-propelled guns.

Many of these tanks and armored vehicles belonged to the Waffen-SS units, the armed portion of Heinrich Himmler's genocidal organization. Beginning as a core battalion of fanatical but relatively inexperienced fighters, by 1943, the Waffen-SS numbered nearly 900,000 men and was a highly skilled and highly motivated force. By the time the Battle of Kursk began, and throughout the rest of the war, the Waffen-SS units would be used as a "fire brigade"—in other words, they were thrown into the front lines where the situation was the direst. Most of the time, they were victorious. When they weren't, they inflicted heavy casualties on the enemy.

By this point in the war, Soviet intelligence had gotten much better in surmising German moves. They also had cultivated important spies and spy rings within Germany and the German army. The Soviets were helped by the codebreaking efforts of the Western Allies, who were able to inform Stalin about many German plans (although the Allies never told them how they found them out). The Soviet reconnaissance forces had gotten much better as well, and the partisan forces had grown to nearly a million. Much information came to the Red Army from behind German lines.

Unbeknownst to Hitler, the Soviets knew about his plans for Kursk almost as soon as he ordered it. In June 1943, they began to create a series of defensive belts in the area, each one more formidable than the last. Millions of mines were sown, thousands of bunkers were built, and thousands of miles of trenches were dug in the Kursk pocket, which encompassed some one hundred miles north to south and about seventy-five miles east to west.

Hitler moved around 70 percent of his tanks and 60 percent of his planes in the Eastern Front to the Kursk area. The German forces numbered between 800,000 to 900,000 men. They had nearly 3,000 tanks and assault guns, 1,800 aircraft, and around 10,000 guns and mortars.

In addition to the unbelievable number of mines, trenches, and other defenses the Soviets prepared, they had anywhere between 1.5

and 1.9 million men, 5,000 tanks, 25,000 guns and mortars, and between 2,700 and 3,500 planes. When they counterattacked, these numbers increased significantly.

The Soviets did not know exactly where the Germans would attack in the Kursk bulge, but they had a pretty good idea. In the north, the Germans planned to attack south of the city of Orel. In the south, they would attack north of Belgorod, hoping the two pincers would link up behind the Soviets at the western end of the bulge and cut them off, just like the old days of 1941.

This was not to be. The Soviets knew almost exactly when the German attack was to begin. To throw the Nazis off, the Red Army began its own massive artillery barrage just before the Germans were to begin theirs. It was a bad omen for the German troops, and it took hours for the men to get organized enough to move forward. Commanding the Soviet effort at Kursk was none other than Marshal Georgy Zhukov, the architect of the defense of Leningrad, Moscow, and Operation Uranus.

However, when the Germans did attack, they initially made good progress, especially in the south. But unlike past battles, where the Germans' initial attacks might progress for weeks or even a month, this one didn't last a week. Though the German Tiger and Panther tanks were superior to the Soviet T-34, that tank had been up-gunned, and the Soviets had much greater numbers. On many occasions, Soviet tanks would not fire on the German Tigers, for even their up-gunned tanks would not make a dent on the German monsters at a distance. Instead, one or more T-34s would ram the Tigers, hoping to damage and immobilize them. And on many occasions, it worked.

Still, for much of the battle, the experienced German tankers made a much heavier dent on the Soviets, but the Reds could afford the losses. The Germans could not. On top of fighting Soviet tanks, the Germans had to defuse or negotiate minefields and massive groups of Soviet anti-tank guns. These guns, especially when up against the

Tigers, would all fire on one tank, destroy it, and then move to the next one.

By July 10th, the German offensive in the north had stalled. Hitler ordered the attack in the south to be reinforced and redoubled. On July 12th, a battle took place near the village of Prokhorovka. This was where the largest tank battle to ever take place occurred.

Illustration 13: Artist's depiction of the battle near Prokhorovka, July 12th, 1943.

At Prokhorovka, the earth literally shook for miles as the German and Soviet tanks took the field. In the area were some 1,400 German and Soviet tanks. On the field of Prokhorovka, 600 Soviet and nearly 300 German armored vehicles charged at each other. They were accompanied by supporting infantrymen and aircraft. Men were blown apart, run over, burned alive, riddled with bullets, and died of smoke inhalation.

When the battle was over, the Soviets had lost more men and tanks, but as a percentage of their forces, the Germans had suffered more, as they could not replace their losses. Hitler called off the offensive for this reason. Also, at the height of the battle, he had gotten word that the Western Allies had invaded Sicily, meaning tanks and men were needed there. It wouldn't have mattered if they stayed.

The Germans were finished on the Eastern Front. For them, there was nothing but the long march back to Berlin.

Bagration

Bagration wasn't a battle: it was an operation that encompassed hundreds of them. Operation Bagration was named after a 19th-century Russian officer in the Imperial Russian Army who became a national hero during the Napoleonic Wars. He actually wasn't Russian—he was Georgian, just like Josef Vissarionovich Dzhugashvili, better known to history as Stalin. This was not a coincidence.

Operation Bagration was the largest offensive undertaken by the Red Army during WWII in both scope and size. It began some three weeks after the Western Allies landed in France and was, in part, meant to draw German troops away from the hard fighting in Normandy.

Bagration began on June 23rd, 1944. More than one and a half million Soviet troops from Leningrad to the borders of southern Belarus attacked the Germans along a front that stretched nearly 700 miles. They were accompanied by 5,800 tanks and assault guns; over 30,000 cannons, rocket launchers, and mortars; and nearly 8,000 aircraft. For comparison, the German assault of 1941 took place on a front of 1,200 miles and included half the number of tanks the Soviets harnessed for Operation Bagration.

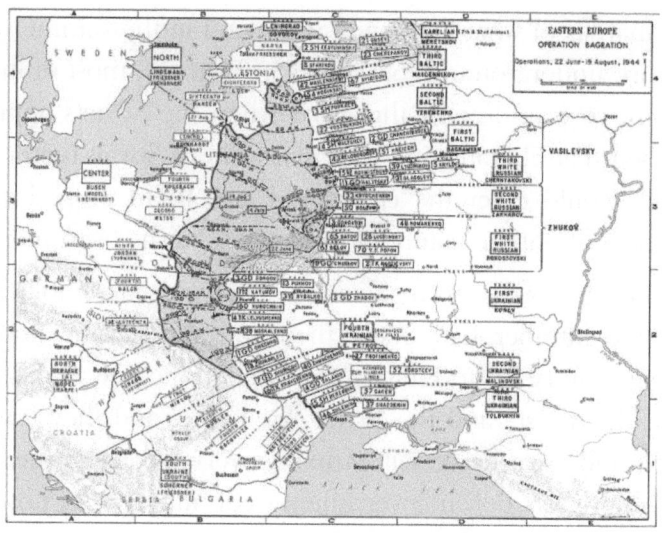

Illustration 14: Operation Bagration was unreal in its scope and size. (Public Domain, https://commons.wikimedia.org/w/index.php?curid=193193).

The Germans faced the Soviet wave with just half a million combat personnel. Support forces numbered another 700,000, and these were picked through to reinforce the front lines (i.e., troops with little or no combat experience). They could only muster 200 functional tanks, 500 assault guns/tank destroyers, 3,300 guns, and just under 1,000 aircraft.

The Soviets attacked in six places in four main army fronts. Despite sustaining heavy casualties because of the Germans' defensive skills, the Soviets pushed the Germans back nearly 400 miles by the end of August. By the time Operation Bagration was over (along with concurrent Soviet offensives in the south into Romania), no German troops were left in the Soviet Union. The Soviets themselves had penetrated Germany itself, as they had pushed into East Prussia and were at the gates of Warsaw, the Polish capital.

This Soviet presence outside Warsaw was an upsetting episode and had consequences for the relationship between the Soviet Union and the Western Allies for years to come. This is not the place for a detailed analysis of what happened in Poland in the summer of 1944, but in short, underground rebel forces in Warsaw, most of them anti-communist, rose up against the Nazis when the Soviets approached. They hoped that liberating their capital without Soviet help or before the Soviets could enter the city would give them more leverage in post-war talks about the nature of the future Polish government.

The Polish forces were divided. Defying incredible odds, a considerable number had made their way to England and France when their country fell to Hitler. Many joined the new "Polish Armed Forces in the West" and the Royal Air Force, and they fought with distinction and great bravery in virtually every theater in the Western Front. The pre-war Polish government went into exile in London and viewed itself as the only legitimate Polish government.

Many other Poles, some by choice, others by necessity, fled to the Soviet Union when the Germans invaded in 1941. At first, these Poles were treated with great suspicion and harshness by Stalin, but as the war turned against him, many Poles were drafted into Polish units of the Red Army. Many also volunteered. They, too, fought with bravery. Many of them were not communists, but a great deal was, and their leaders certainly were. They fully intended to dominate post-war Poland after the war.

Stalin ordered his troops to stop their advance at the River Vistula just across from Warsaw. Truth be told, many Red Army units were exhausted and depleted. However, there were more than enough units to take the fight into Warsaw to help the Poles. Additionally, nothing was stopping the Soviet air force from dropping supplies in Warsaw and bombing the Germans. But nothing happened. Britain and the United States pleaded with Stalin to aid the Poles or allow them to fly supplies in, which they could have easily done. However, Stalin denied them landing rights in areas under Soviet control, which many of them would have needed.

So, the Red Army watched as the Nazis destroyed the Polish 1944 Uprising. Warsaw was flattened; literally 90 percent of the buildings in the capital were wiped out. Thousands of anti-communist Poles were killed, which was just what Stalin wanted. It was not until January 1945, when the Soviets began their final offensive, that they entered the city. At Yalta, both Winston Churchill and Franklin D. Roosevelt had to face facts and realize that nothing was going to remove Stalin from Poland.

Berlin

The Battle of Berlin, like the other battles described here, deserves its own book. Thousands have been written on the subject already, but we'll give you a brief outline of the battle that ended WWII in Europe for our purposes here.

The battle for the Nazi capital began on April 16th, 1945, four days before Hitler's fifty-sixth birthday. By this time, Hitler was a drug-addled and crazed semblance of the man he was when the war began. He was living in a bunker far below the city center with a coterie of Nazi Party leaders, notably Propaganda Minister Joseph Goebbels and his family and Party Secretary Martin Bormann. Along for the end was Hitler's girlfriend, Eva Braun, whom he married on April 29th.

The Soviets likely could have begun the battle for the capital in February, but the Yalta Conference was held from February 4th to the 11th. This conference was a meeting between Stalin, Roosevelt, and Churchill in the Crimean city of the same name, which had been called to discuss post-war Europe and the world. Many troublesome questions needed to be answered before the final stages of the war began in the spring, and one of them was who was going to take Berlin.

Though there has been some debate on whether the Western Allies could have driven on to the German capital, it was made clear at Yalta that the honor would fall to the Soviets. Of the three Great Powers, they were the only country that had been invaded by Hitler. An astounding 90 percent of all German military casualties took place in the fight against the Red Army. On the other hand, over twenty million Soviets had died or been killed due to the Nazi invasion.

Many people do not know this, but the Red Army units fought each other for the right to be the first troops into the Reichstag (the German parliament). Imagine what might have happened had British or American troops been there.

By April 25th, the city was surrounded. Berlin had basically been razed to the ground by the American and British bombing campaigns, but the Soviets were going to make sure the Germans were not only defeated but also got a taste of their own medicine. It is estimated that around the city of Berlin, which was not a small city by any means, the Soviets had nearly 30,000 artillery pieces and mortars—one every ten yards around the city—that were rows deep. When the final barrage began, the Soviet artillery would have been seen from space.

Inside Berlin, the SS, the fanatical shock troops of the Nazi movement, began a terror campaign against anyone they believed to have shirked their duty or deserted. Hundreds, if not thousands, of Germans were shot. Many were hanged from trees, light posts, or makeshift gallows, with their bodies left to rot with signs around their necks saying things like, "I am a filthy traitor and have betrayed the Führer and Fatherland!" Some of these victims were teenagers and women.

The youth branch of the Nazi Party, the Hitler Youth, was armed. Children as young as ten were sent to the front lines. Old men and wounded veterans made their way there as well as part of the *Volkssturm* ("People's Storm"). Armed with the effective anti-tank *Panzerfaust*, these ill-trained troops managed to inflict many casualties on the Soviet units. In turn, many of these German forces were wiped out completely.

When the Soviets entered the city, intense street fighting began. For a few days, savage battles took place all over the city—in the streets, shells of buildings, and sewers. Sometimes, surrendering Germans would be taken as prisoners. Sometimes, they fought to the last bullet and killed themselves with it, as did civilians all over Germany, for they believed the Allies would kill the men and rape the women. Other times, surrendering Germans were killed on the spot. It really was an odds game.

Before the battle began, the Soviets went on a rampage throughout the liberated areas of eastern Germany. Villages were burnt to the ground. Tens, maybe hundreds of thousands, of German women and girls were raped, with many killed afterward, either by the Germans or their own hand. Atrocities were widespread, and they only increased every time the Soviets discovered a German extermination camp on their march westward. By the time they got to Berlin, what Soviet propaganda often called "The Lair of the Beast," many Red Army troops went berserk. During the battle and for days afterward, raping and killing were the orders for the day. The Soviet high command looked the other way but ordered it to stop after some weeks went by. This was not done out of pity, but because it was becoming counterproductive to Soviet post-war plans to occupy the eastern part of Germany, as had been agreed at Yalta.

When the Battle of Berlin was over, the Germans had over 100,000 dead. The Soviets had an equal number. Nearly 500,000 German troops were taken prisoner, and many never returned. About 25,000 German civilians were killed as a result of the fighting. One of them was Adolf Hitler, who gave a cyanide capsule to his wife, Eva, before shooting himself in the temple.

WWII in Europe officially ended on May 8th, 1945, with the formal surrender of the German armed forces and Hitler's designated successor, Admiral Karl Dönitz.

Illustration 15: Red Army soldiers tossing captured Nazi banners to the ground in Red Square, Moscow, 1945.

Conclusion

The war in Europe ended in May 1945. According to an agreement reached with Roosevelt at Yalta, Stalin declared war on Japan two months after Germany's defeat. All along the Soviet borders with China, Manchuria, and Korea, Soviet troops attacked the Japanese Imperial Army, which still numbered a million troops.

It was no contest as to who was the strongest. The Japanese had no fight left in them. The Americans were closing in on the Japanese Home Islands, and millions of Chinese and other Asian peoples, who had been held down by the Japanese for years, were about to be at their throats. The Soviets marched in with ease. They occupied the Kurile Islands and the formerly divided (between the USSR and Japan) Sakhalin Island to the north of Japan. It appeared that they might try to invade the northernmost Japanese island of Hokkaido as well—at least that was a fear of the Americans.

The atomic bombs dropped on Hiroshima and Nagasaki stopped all that. Though some scholars and others on the Left have said the US used the bombs to dissuade the Soviets from any further moves in Asia and China, that was not the case. The bomb was dropped to defeat Japan, but dissuading the Soviets was certainly a positive side-effect, at least from an American political point of view.

The Soviet Union, despite not having the atomic bomb (it would develop its own in 1949), was now one of two world "superpowers." Its army was the biggest in the world, though its strategic air force and navy were dwarfed by the US forces. Still, Eastern Europe was firmly under Soviet control, and despite Stalin's pledges to hold "free elections" in nations occupied by his armies, those free elections never happened. In the Baltic states, Poland, Czechoslovakia, Romania, Hungary, Bulgaria, and eastern Germany (which became the German Democratic Republic in 1949), Soviet armies backed home-grown Stalin-approved communists. Only one Eastern European nation of any size remained independent of the Soviets: Yugoslavia. Numerous partisan forces had liberated their country, and their leader, Josip Broz Tito, was firmly against Stalin's demands.

Still, the USSR itself was a disaster. The war set the nation back years. The population didn't achieve pre-war levels until the end of the 1950s. The economy did not come back until then or even later. Even today, the war is remembered not only as a great victory but also as an inhuman catastrophe. To this day, the leaders of Russia are extraordinarily suspicious of the West and zealous about guarding their borders.

Of course, between the end of WWII and 1991, the US and the USSR "fought" the Cold War, a conflict using proxy armies, politics, economics, propaganda, spying, assassinations, and much more. For a time in the 1990s, the world thought this was a part of the past. With the arrival of Vladimir Putin, who is very much a student of history, a new Cold War has begun.

Here's another book by Captivating History that you might be interested in

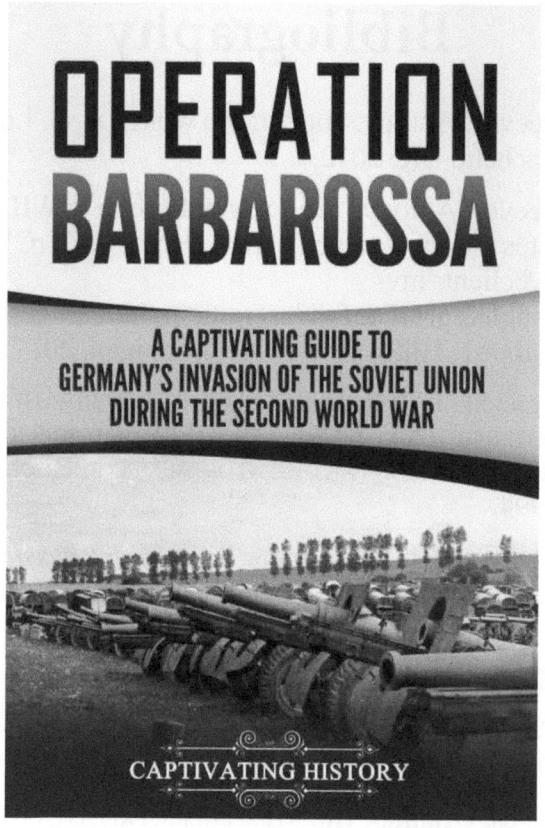

Bibliography

Beevor, Antony. THE SECOND WORLD WAR. London: Hachette UK, 2012.

Beevor, Antony. "The Soviet Role in WWII." Lecture, https://www.youtube.com/watch?v=AZErCVlIDJg&hl=id&client=mv-google&gl=ID&fulldescription=1&app=desktop&persist_app=1, Hillsdale College, Michigan, 2017.

Berezhkov, Valentin M. AT STALIN'S SIDE: HIS INTERPRETER'S MEMOIRS FROM THE OCTOBER REVOLUTION TO THE FALL OF THE DICTATOR'S EMPIRE. Birch Lane Press, 1994.

Bellamy, Chris. *Absolute War: Soviet Russia in the Second World War*. 2008

Clark, Lloyd. KURSK: THE GREATEST BATTLE. London: Hachette UK, 2013.

Conquest, Robert. THE GREAT TERROR: A REASSESSMENT. Oxford: Oxford University Press on Demand, 2008.

Figes, Orlando. THE WHISPERERS: PRIVATE LIFE IN STALIN'S RUSSIA. London: Penguin UK, 2008.

Fitzpatrick, Sheila. *EVERYDAY STALINISM: ORDINARY LIFE IN EXTRAORDINARY TIMES: SOVIET RUSSIA IN THE 1930S*. New York: Oxford University Press, USA, 2000.

Herman, Victor. COMING OUT OF THE ICE: AN UNEXPECTED LIFE. 1979.

McSherry, James. STALIN, HITLER, AND EUROPE: THE ORIGINS OF WORLD WAR II, 1933-1939. 1968.

Merridale, Catherine. *Ivan's War: Life and Death in the Red Army, 1939-1945.* 2007.

Topitsch, Ernst. STALIN'S WAR: A RADICAL NEW THEORY OF THE ORIGINS OF THE SECOND WORLD WAR. New York: St. Martin's Press, 1987.

Volkogonov, Dmitriĭ A. STALIN: TRIUMPH AND TRAGEDY. New York: Grove Weidenfeld, 1991.

Werth, Alexander. *Russia at War, 1941–1945: A History.* 2017.

Printed by
Libri Plureos GmbH · Friedensallee 273
22763 Hamburg · Germany